DEAD IN THE
PEWS

Dead in the Pews

Dr. Jatendra McCray

2911 Publishing, Inc.

Contents

2911 Publishing Inc., 2020

Dedication

God, thank you for this gift and your unconditional love; thank you for not allow.   ing me to give up not matter how many times I tried to throw in the towel.

My late Grandmother, Constance Bernice Jenkins, a prayer warrior, encourager   and my personal pusher in my walk with God, education and life.

My late Uncle-Cousin Bishop Walter Leigh Bates for your example and leadership. Some of his last words to me were to push me to complete this book and I am ever so grateful. We had many conversations about life, theology, business, etc., during which he certainly planted seeds and left a legacy.

There are too many friends, family, leaders and the like who remain active in my life and have inspired me along the way, so I dare not begin to name and miss someone, except one:

Derrick Jr., my son, my reason, my gift from God. I love you!

Introduction

There is a state of emergency in churches everywhere. The church, also known as the spiritual "hospital," has become a haven for the dead and dying, in lieu of a place to go to be revived, refreshed, and renewed. The world today has adopted a trend that is inclusive of pseudo-reality, smokescreens, and facades in an attempt to escape the need to face the facts; sadly, this epidemic is exactly what has spread into some of the Houses of God.

This is not a book to bash the church in any way, shape, or form, but rather to enlighten us as a people to realize who we are. The corporate church is a place that simply needs to get back to the way that God originally intended for it to be. Due to the multi-factorial hurt and dying souls the reputation of the church is undoubtedly greatly affected. My prayer is that bringing healing to the people that make up the corporate church, will bring the restoration and revival we so desperately need to sanctuaries everywhere.

The matters of pseudo-reality in both the world and the church really have more in common than one would think. When a person avoids what their truth is, it is not often because they have a burning desire to lie or deceive others, but rather mask what their reality is because facing it hurts. For many, facing the truth is painful and it forces us to confront some things that we never wanted to see again. If you cannot face your own past, or be real with your present, you render yourself incapable of helping another face and conquer their own. A failure to own your past will hinder your present and delay your arrival to the future. Additionally, when we cannot or do not face "us" we limit God's transforming power in our lives to heal, deliver and set free.

We must remember that we have a common denominator; we are people who have issues, fears, hard times and some of the same sins of the past and present. As runners in the same race ultimately attempting to reach the same goal, our overall focus should be to ensure that everyone makes it to the finish line. In this race for our lives we cannot afford casualties of war. Keep in mind that there is one enemy who has one sole goal — that we all give up, stumble, and fall to eventually live eternally in a lake of fire and brimstone. What can we do collectively to help this bitter end be avoided?

This book is not just for the "church people". This book is to every single person who has been to church, desired to come church, left the church and is in the church now DYING. Outside of the church this is for everyone who has ever found themselves lost or in a place of giving up; essentially, this inspired literature is for everyone. My endeavor is that this book reaches the leaders and lay members alike, as well as those who can't find themselves in / or out of the church. My prayer is that you find yourself or someone you know in these pages and find the inspiration to live again. My hope is, that as painful as it may be, you find the strength and courage to face what has been holding you captive and choose today to allow God to break the chains in your life. You deserve to live, you are entitled to be free and you have too much potential to be dead in the pews.

The only death that we are admonished or required to take on is that of being "Dead in Christ" when we become dead to the deeds of the flesh and dead therefore to sin (Romans 8:9-11). When we become dead in Christ we receive life that we could not have experienced while living selfishly in sin, walking to the beat of our own drum. The truth is until you accept that at some point you will have to die to yourself, you have not in fact lived, you've existed. We must give away our will, habits, shortcomings and doubt in exchange for the purpose we were created to fulfill.

The death that I speak of in the coming chapters is not literal but figurative; Oddly enough, this figurative death will be become very real in a natural and spiritual sense unless one is truly healed. Healing comes by facing yourself and everything that comes with that package-a combination of not just facing your issue, but seeking and pursuing relief, deliverance and release by any means necessary. No one chooses death as an initial option, however, the longer you live in the past and entertain the inability to move forward, dying becomes seemingly inevitable, and at times the only option. If one is not careful, the snares of death can entrap you before you realize you are on the path to destruction. This death is in the form of discouragement sent by the enemy to distract you from your purpose in life. Make up in your mind now that you will be committed to live. Yes, you do have a choice! The reality is some things are meant to die to, but not be found dead in.

I have been in every place this book will take you. I am speaking to you from my heart and as I am encouraged to write each word I am praying for those that will turn these pages. We need more people healed so the churches can rise up to the call to heal, set free, and deliver those we are mandated to compel to come in. Open you heart and clear your mind. I pray that after reading this book, your life will never be the same again! There is too much life in you to allow your past to force you to give up.

Let's deal with the things that have been contributing factors in life that may cause us to feel as if we are in a dead space.

1

The Life Factor

Everybody has a pew — a circumstance, story, situation, trial, or never ending saga of one's truth that we've sat on at some point in life. Your pew may not look like another's but it exists nonetheless. We as people are a mélange of who / what we are, do, go through, and how we react, all fitting into the equation of who we are destined to be. It is after riding this course that suddenly, life happens, awakening a chain of events of sorts that being ill-prepared for seems, at best, the closest we'll ever be to "ready".

When does life not throw a curveball? That, of course, is a rhetorical question. Life is often full of surprises including ups, downs, highs, lows, peaks & valleys, much of which is out of our control. Some things we go through can be avoided, some are necessary, and others are inevitable. It is the events of life that shape us into the person we become and mold us into the person we were born to be. It is often the pressures of living that causes us to change in ways that we thought we never would, either good or bad, often a product of our environment versus producing from the environment we are in. Forrest Gump ™ said, "Life is like a box of chocolates;,you never know what you're going to get." While the statement is true, there are two ways to look at it before forming a conclusion. Boxes of chocolate are usually filled with more of what we don't like, the favorites being few and far between. Life, like that box of candy will be full of things (moments) we don't like or particularly have a taste for. We can go through life tasting the pieces, spitting them out and throwing them away or, we can accept them for what they are and learn to live with the chocolate we have been given with the outlook that something good must be inside. Remember that some things in life appear one way and taste another, therefore, we cannot live life based off appearances alone. The results we see in life are based on more on the choices we make than the factors we see.

It's safe to say that's a place we have all been at one point or another where we were faced with negativity, resentfulness, sadness and even bitterness. Often times, instead of looking at the things we go through and trying to find purpose in them, we feel punished and deserving of a better or different life altogether, yet remain stagnant versus pursuit of change. When life happens, and it will, your reaction means everything to your next step into your future. You can choose to be beat up, broken, and in despair or you can learn lessons and use each obstacle as a stepping stone to get where you need to be. As hard as it gets at times, never forget that giving up is not an option. None of us are here merely by chance; every day you are awake, your beating heart proof that there is another chance to fulfill your purpose. One lesson life has taught me is that there is no true life outside of the will of God; an attempt to live outside of your identity in Christ is purposeless existence. If you stopped here because you believe in "a creator" or " a being", or you believe there is a God but you don't formally worship Him, I encourage you to read on; You were not manufactured, you were created, thus getting to know the depths of your creation and Creator are vital to you being the best version of yourself.

I have met many dead people in my life. Having been in a similar pair of shoes, I recognize the dead both near and far. Death has a unique scent that often reveals itself before physically seen, being inimitable in odor that cannot be disguised, ignored, nor easily forgotten. The stench of death carries a distinction that cannot be masked and a presence that can be misconstrued but never denied. Would you believe it if I told you that you sit next to dead people often? People are dead at home, school, the stores, and in the church. I am not speaking of people who have died a physical or natural death but rather one that is emotional, mental, or spiritual in nature. So many people merely exist, but they do not have much life left in them. This is the result of life happening and one not knowing how to deal with it, so they don't deal at all. When you ignore a thing it does not cease to be, but rather it remains hidden, looked over, and trampled upon. Your issues have a lifeline as long as they exist because they are attached to you. As long as you refuse to deal with the matters plaguing you they will consistently drain you of the life you give to them until you make a decision to face them, cut the umbilical cord, and LIVE. Issues go away when we stop subscribing to their installments; cancel the attachment it has to you and without a viable source it is sure to perish.

There are people that have died natural, real death due to a failure to find seek, find, or attain a way beyond their pew. How, you might ask? Stress, depression, hopelessness, suppression of emotion and loss of will can manifest into physical sickness in your body; once there is a living root, what sprouts or produces is largely up to you. You must confront your reality before it opposes you to the point of wavering to the losing side. There are two types of agents; catalysts and antagonists. You will either be the change agent that the catalyst so proudly exudes or you will find yourself changed and altered by everything you encounter, as such is the life of the antagonist. When your issues find you, they come with a vengeance and offer no route for escape. The things that we see as normal or inevitable such as stress, worry, anger, and strife are the very things that kill. It took some time, talking with God, and facing some real pain before I made the decision to live. I went through times of giving up, my mind was plagued with thoughts of suicide and bouts of depression, and I sometimes found myself hoping life would painlessly, miraculously end for me. In retrospect, I didn't really want to die – I just didn't want to live in pain, while at the time blinded by my smokescreen and seeing few options to change. I did not want to be forced to face the very things that I blamed for getting me where I was at that point in my life. I blamed my upbringing, relationships that didn't work out, rape / molestation, divorce, and others for everything that transpired. It was then that I decided to look at my box of chocolates a little differently because clearly, bitterly tasting and throwing everything away just was not working.

Two very important factors can completely change your outlook on your life – perception and trust. Your perception is merely how you choose to see through the thoughts in your mind. While you cannot control destiny and the factors that led up to that point, you can control your outlook, reactions, and your view. If you see the things experienced as negative, the chances that you will react as such or expect a less than favorable outcome than if you were to turn those thoughts for the positive is increased. The trust factor comes in when we seek to gain an understanding of why we go experience the things we do. We do not experience tests and trials to break us down but rather to build us up. Our tests are one of the ways that God shows us how much he trusts us. Sounds crazy right? Before jumping to that conclusion, think about how many people did not survive the things that you have been through. How many times were you strengthened to outlive the thing you thought came to take you out? When God can trust us to be faithful and endure in the midst of our world seemingly falling apart, we become candidates for the promise! God doesn't trust everyone with a testimony; in knowing this, the enemy will do everything to cause us to fold before we come to the realization that we can still win with a bad hand. When in doubt about the process, be encouraged by the promise!

You might be reading this and thinking this does not apply to you because no one has been through what you have. Perhaps no one has had to face the amount of pain, betrayal, and loss that you have. It is even possible that you feel as if no one in the world could ever understand. I submit to you that someone does understand. There is a God in Heaven that knows every hair on your head, every breath that you take, and every move you will make. Even when we choose not to believe in Him, he's never given up on us; more so many in this world do not know Him at all, but it changes his existence and love for us no less.

Luke 12:7 - But even the very hairs of your head are all numbered. Fear not therefore: you are of more value than many sparrows.

Jeremiah 1:5 - Before you were in the womb I knew you. (paraphrase)

Nothing that we go through surprises God. We often feel misunderstood because we first choose not to understand; often times we fight or avoid what we do not comprehend or what we are convicted by. As cliché as it may sound, everything really does happen for a reason. Life has a not so funny way of putting things into perspective if we wait for outcome. When you begin to lay your problems out and seek to understand the purpose behind them you will begin to see life differently. Some divorce to experience true love; others must go through abandonment to realize what acceptance, need, want, and fulfilled desires really means. What if someone else is depending on your going through and making it so they won't give up? For as much as we have a picture of how our life should or could be, the reality is we cannot choose our destiny; freewill enables us to make decisions that can affect how we get to it, but only disobedience can deter us from it.

Life is far from a fairy tale. If I have learned anything, it is that my life, though far from perfect, has been full of necessary events that have pushed me to my present place. I have not always understood and I do not have it all together, but I, like you, am more than a conqueror. Although it seems as if it would be so much better if life were "easy" we will later read about the beauty that comes from the ugliest of circumstances. Life is full of opportunities disguised as trials and tribulations to make you into the person you're intended to be. We tend to hide behind the good things and avoid the bad altogether when in fact you need them both to make it. A race without hurdles and obstacles doesn't give you much to look forward to; the goal or prize would not be worth as much if it was easily attained. It is the unexpected leaps, ducks, dodges and dives that make reaching the finish line worthwhile. Working out doesn't yield optimal results without going through the motions of conditioning, training, resistance, and endurance. Winning results, while not instantaneous, are always worth it. We must come to the realization that though it hurt, pain got us here today; wallowing in the pity is a choice, not a requirement. Giving up the right to hold on to pain will grant you access to the purpose predestined for your life.

In a seemingly perfect world many would ideally like to never go through or they would have the ability to choose what they experience. If we all had the option to choose our tests and trials, realistically we'd choose to always be on the mountaintop and never have a valley experience. The valley shows you who and what you are, what is in you that must come out, who you can truly rely on and most importantly tenacity and will that you may have before, not known you have within. If you were always on the mountaintop you'd forget the beauty and serene tranquility of the valley, and if stuck on the plains of the low place you'd take for granted the height of the mountain and what it takes to make it to the peak. The valley is a low place surrounded by goals to attain and purpose to complete! Don't let the mountains intimidate you — speak to them, find a way to climb and conquer them one at a time.

The life of the Eagle

The greatest accomplishments in a Bald Eagle's lifetime are perhaps those fears and feats they overcome in the valley. During the molting process, a necessary stage in life, the Eagle is faced with losing to win or existing to die. There comes a time when what at one time was life-sustaining, has now become a threat to its very existence, unless it is willing to go through the painful process of losing it all to change, grow, and come back better than before. Once feared by many and revered by others, the Eagle is now vulnerable and at risk to be preyed upon, especially if it loses sight of the necessity of the process. The woes of can easily be compared to our walk in life in our very own processes.

For the Eagle its plumage is directly linked to its survival as a species, having functions to protect, insulate, transport in flight and give its unique, often enamored, identity a distinct appearance. When molting begins, the feathers now not as useful, weighed down with dirt, debris, oil, and brokenness, must be pulled out or fall out in order to be replaced by new growth. The process of losing something so long a part of you which has now become your individuality can be hard; the fear of being naked and vulnerable in front of those you once stood so proudly before can be a daunting reality to face. There comes a point in life where we must shed the image, reputation, thoughts, patterns, and even façade of who people have made us, to walk into the person we were created to become. When we get rid of what is weighing us down, we find success in flight and an ability to soar beyond our ability and be greater than we could have ever imagined. Each layer of growth that we must so patiently await, will interlock as that of the design on the Eagle, in stages that teach us lessons so vital to apply in the days, months, and years to come. Just as growth in life, each layer of feathers will serve a purpose as they come together to help us flourish, fly, and succeed.

The Eagle loses the ability to create tears in the eyes, due to the clogging of the tear ducts, causing it to temporarily lose its envied sharpness in vision. The Eagle's temporary loss of sharp vision is a reminder that we must use our INsight to see only what is necessary to learn, grow, and of course, survive. While our natural sight is blurry we must rely on discernment to allow us to see the necessary and rely more on our other senses to survive. Everything is not meant to be seen, and what is, is often overlooked due to our lack of focus or selective seeing, again, in our effort to mask our reality. At times we may find it easier to not see, thus avoiding pain, until at some point what we have avoided becomes our biggest competition. What we choose to not see or what we focus on that should be overlooked, has a way of confronting us down the road to bring into peripheral perspective the reality we must face. The road may get blurry from time to time, but with focus and passion, your vision can and will come back like the Eagle's, sharper than before once healing has taken place.

The strong beak, the Eagle's key to survival and tool to catch, devour prey, and remain nourished, becomes calcified in the molting process rendering him weak. In times like these we must find ourselves not relying on our ability to survive on our own will / power but tap into the source we find in God to provide us with all we need to make it through the chapters of our lives. As the process ends, the Eagle, now equipped with new feathers finds a rock in a high place to hit its beak on, painfully breaking the calcium off, fracturing its strongest attribute but ultimately once again finding the strength to live. There are some things that you will have to break off to get to the next level; when you tap into your ability to lose without losing and let go of what is hurting you, only then can you truly understand and relish in what it takes to win and sustain victory.

At the most daunting point of the process, an older, more mature Eagle will fly over the valley where the molting Eagle is to yell what seems to be encouragement and to drop food / nourishment so they have something to sustain them in their low place. You must survive because while the molting Eagle may be you now, or may have been in the past, the mature Eagle in you will be next in season helping someone else! Do not allow pride to intrude in your season of growth and cause you to be unavailable or unreceptive to nourishment from others in your valley experience. Moreover, while you may, at times, wish to shirk the responsibility, you must survive to help someone else not die in what you survived.

The process is often painful, and at times seemingly less than worth it; the end product of newness, growth, potential and destiny reminds us why going through is necessary. It is difficult to get to the light at the end of the tunnel when plagued by doubt and darkness along the way. A passageway is never single sided – to get through to the other side there is a course to get to the end where results wait as the reward for the experience. Once the Eagle has gone through, it finds in its first flight a renewed ability to soar against the wind, a restoration of its sharp vision as tears clean the temporary blindness away, and a tenacity to live like never before. Enduring the regrowth and making it through the molting is essential to move beyond existing to the realm of living, soaring heights and depths, transformations, and living experiences that you once never thought you would see. If the Eagle chooses not to molt, it seals its fate to exist, fail to live, and eventually die never reaching its full potential. Regardless of how it looks, how much it hurts, and the loneliness we may at times feel we must molt to move beyond the place we are in. Jeremiah 18:1 reminds us of the importance of staying in the potter's hands while on the wheel of life. Being molded and made does not feel good and may require brokenness and remodeling, but it's necessary.

We are trained by the trials that we face. Trials not only build patience and endurance, but they also serve to help us gain experience as well as provide lessons that we must learn from to carry us throughout our journey. Conditioning and endurance go hand in hand as we are fueled by the heaviness and trials that lie ahead; it's at these times that we are called to push through despite the weight, endure the hurt and the pain, thereby succeeding at all costs. Without ambition the race is as good as lost. Ambition says that regardless of how much farther there is to go, what is facing me in this run, and in spite of what obstacles I incur and hurdles I will jump, I am determined to see the goal. Treat life like the race that you are determined to finish!

If life was in fact perfect, it wouldn't be worth living. Why? If we never had difficulties to face, we would become a people that put ourselves above God and move beyond our need for his unconditional love, grace, and mercy. What makes life constant is the variable of inevitable unpredictability that we experience. It's what happens between the "Once upon a time" and "Happily ever after" that makes your story just what it is. Living in the dash is what makes life what it is. Expecting everything to always go according to a set plan is nice, but it is not realistic. We must remember that our lives are not our own, keeping in mind that every day is filled with new mercy and grace to attain the purpose we were created for.

When life throws you a curveball don't get hit and knocked down; catch the ball and use it to your advantage. Use every opportunity presented to you as the drive to become a better you. You must not die until you have fulfilled your purpose on this Earth. There is no room for regret in your future. We have all done things that we are less than proud of. Use those experiences as lessons and move on with your life. Don't allow things that have transpired in the past to kill you in your NOW. Your past is just that for a reason; looking past time that has passed is needed to walk into your current to build on the future.

Focus on getting where you need to be, to get where you need to go. There is no hater in this world that can do more damage to you, then you can do to yourself. The biggest enemy in our lives is often found within; we tend to focus on the things going wrong, mistakes made, failures, pain, etc., and allow that to distract us from our purpose. Often times we critique our self before anyone else has the chance. Now is your chance to speak life to yourself. Now is the time to encourage yourself and be your biggest motivator. Appreciate life for what it is now because you cannot smell the roses once you are dead. Life is going to happen with or without your consent– what you do with it and how you live it is a choice only you can make.

Be determined to be a storm chaser – get to it, grow through it and move on! Don't allow storms to run you out of your promised place. In the natural there are people who chase down storms to get the first shots of the destruction on a play by play basis as well as the aftermath. The key is not getting so caught up in the storm that you get stuck and more damage is suffered than intended. Storms come to make you, not to kill you. In the spiritual, storms come and go, as we go through different things in our life. Don't just sit there and wallow in the puddle and get accustomed to the storms as they come and go; Seek God concerning the origin of the storm, watch and be prayerful concerning what the storm comes to take away or add to, and no matter the aftermath be grateful. In both the natural and spiritual storms never come without reason. When a storm is on the horizon it comes to bring water to a place that is dry or in need of nourishment; it also comes to uproot everything without a stable foundation. Do not lose track of God in the storm! The key to surviving is remaining rooted and grounded.

Purpose is waiting for you to make the choice to live. God has predestined a plan for our lives that surpasses any dream we have for ourselves, but we must walk in faith and hope to get there. Looking back will cause you to procrastinate moving forward. You are right on track and if you feel as if you are off, now is the time to jump back on while the train is moving! No time has been lost! Your life is making you who you were destined to be – trials, tribulations, triumphs and all; Live and move FORWARD!

2

The Truth about
"Church hurt"

This is perhaps the most controversial chapter in this book, because it dissects and challenges one of the greatest issues plaguing the church today — "church hurt."; a term not deemed as favorable, but a tangible experience for many to say the least. This hurt from a church comes in more forms than one can name, disguised as betrayal, offense, defense, damage caused by the flawed integrity and character of one or lack thereof, abandonment of families in the name of ministry and more. The list of hurts from the church continues to grow as the offenses continue to be counted, putting the place that is not keeping score on the defense, at the losing end of the battle with more TKOs than one can count. While church hurt may not be *your* experience its reality to many should not be discounted or thrown away. Why? What we don't face that starts as a primary intention / simple wound festers, gets infected and creates larger, more deadly wounds with a deadly diagnosis due to lack of exposure, cleaning, change and follow up care.

So often have we heard and seen those mortally wounded by the deeds of those found in the one place they hoped to come, be healed, and made whole. Like the box of chocolates most of us look the same on the outside, but the reality that we have different consistencies, weight, and ability to withstand pressure is evident. Many times, the things that one can handle or "get over", another is blindsided by, at times, never to recover. Countless people are plagued and guilt ridden by deeds committed that have marked them like a scarlet letter, forever labeling them as less than, unforgivable, or without purpose — none of which is like the God of mercy, grace, unconditional love and forgiveness that we have come to know.

The reality is that it is not the *church* that hurts. There are things that we go through in and around the church that seemingly affect our relationship with the church and ultimately the way that we see, and reverence, God. Why is it that the things that affect us naturally tend to cause us to venture away from the spiritual side of our lives? While there is a direct connection between the natural and spiritual, in that the things we take in naturally can either taint or build our spiritual being, how we overcome or are overtaken affects our relationship with God. Many times God is seen and expected to be the savior, even of people who forsake Him and His will, ending with the creator taking the blame for the something the creation has done. Man is man and God is God, and we must not confuse the ability, intention, or character of the two.

The hurt that we delve into has often been at the hands of those seen as direct representation of God, bringing to the surface the inquiry as to *why God doesn't intervene or how certain things are allowed to happen.* Just as God uses man to do His work in the Earth, Satan does as well, causing many to stand and profess Jesus with their mouths, while living lives of pride, egoism, hidden motives, unhealed incidences they then project on others and more; these profess Jesus but cannot worship in spirit and truth nor confess with their hearts because they serve two Masters - one with their mouth and one with their heart. In other instances people have been hurt by those who do not have ill intentions, resulting nonetheless in a gaping wound.

Church hurt is a term that has been around for generations and beyond. Truly, this hurt existed, before the term was coined into existence. Those that are most hurt in situations like these are they who come in to the church with expectations for what the church is and who the church contains and find themselves sorely disappointed. There must be an understanding, first, of what the church really is. The meaning of the church is two-fold. First and foremost, the temple / sanctuary is the place that God has set apart and consecrated for His use, much like a hospital of sorts where we come to fellowship and be healed. The corporate church is the place we gather physically for the sake of worship, prayer, fellowship, teaching and encouragement (See Hebrews 10:25).

Hebrews 10:25 - Not forsaking the assembling of ourselves together, as the manner of some is; but exhorting one another: and so much the more, as ye see the day approaching.

The universal church is us, made up of everyone who has received salvation and is a believer of Jesus Christ; God has imparted the same work that church was created to do within us so that we might be the church — a temple of agape love, healing and restoration — wherever we go to complete His work within the Earth. The church is not technically a place, a building, a denomination or a specific set of beliefs. The church is allowed to be the church when we go out into the world as we were called and created to do which is known as the Great Commission (Matthew 28:18-20) (Luke 14:23) The universal church is best referred to and widely known as the Body of Christ.

Matthew 28:18-20 [18] And Jesus came and spake unto them, saying, All power is given unto me in heaven and in earth.

[19] Go ye therefore, and teach all nations, baptizing them in the name of the Father, and of the Son, and of the Holy Ghost:

[20] Teaching them to observe all things whatsoever I have commanded you: and, lo, I am with you always, even unto the end of the world. Amen.

Luke 14:23 - And the lord said unto the servant, Go out into the highways and hedges, and compel them to come in, that my house may be filled.

Having dissected what the church actually is opens up the topic of church hurt even further for our understanding. We must understand that we are human beings above all else. Though our being human is a reality it is not an open door of excuses for our behavior and the way that we choose to live our lives. Due to Satan originating sin first by way of envy and pride (Isaiah 14:12-17) and introducing sin to Adam and Eve in the Garden of Eden (Genesis 3:1-17) as the serpent, our human nature was directly affected, which is why Jesus Christ came to die for our sins. Jesus Christ did not just die for past sins as well as those being committed when He walked the Earth, but He also gave His life for those to come who He knew, due to our nature, would make mistakes and live lives replicate of a sinful nature until we make the choice to give up our will and accept His to live a life free from sin and bondage. Psalm 51:5 reads, *Behold I was shapen in iniquity and in sin did my mother conceive me.* This is not indicative of the very act of conception but rather the state of the human race in that we are all sinners until we are saved by grace.

Romans 3:23 – For all have sinned and fallen short of the glory of God.

The fact is that in a real church you will encounter real people with real issues. How or why? Because that is what the church is for. The church, like the hospital, is the place for the diseased, desperate, low and in despair without another option for help. If you walk into a church where there is never a need for healing or deliverance, run in the opposite direction. If everyone in the church is perfect, the purpose is not being fulfilled as the church must be a filling station of healing, confession, discipling, growth and compelling in a never ending cycle. The church as God intended is a place to change lives, not recycle catchy phrases / slogans, teach the same sermons, recycle saintly members and praise all day without life changing encounters with our Creator, God. The issue comes in with church hurt because we presumably walk into a perfect place with imperfect standards and get upset with a less than perfect outcome. Nothing beautiful starts out that way; anything worth having is worth waiting for *and* if there is no pain, there is no gain. We have heard these things that have become clichés over the years, but actually realizing them to be true is something altogether different.

It's interesting that while in the world or running the streets when we are hurt we call it life, but within the confines of the church some associate it with God and never recover. Ironically, we don't hear of people severing ties with employers, relationships, and the things that cause them hurt in life as often as many feel entitled to cut God off due to what is experienced in a building, absent the influence of the true and living God. Do not allow anything or anyone to have so much power over you that their actions cause you to miss God and abandon the call for your life. As long as there is life, the threat and realistic end to the satanic kingdom gets closer and closer each day. We were never promised that life would be a fairytale. What we were promised is eternal life, if we meet the standard of holiness, and live according to the BIBLE (**B**asic **I**nstructions **B**efore **L**eaving **E**arth).

There is the expectation that one would not come to the church and suffer hurt or disappointment of any kind because of it being the house of God. Honestly, we shouldn't find gossip, lying, cheating, and immorality in the sanctuary, however, imperfections will be found wherever people are because there is no perfect human being. We cannot expect deity to manifest from mortality. Coming to the church with the expectation that it will be perfect is likened to walking into a hospital and expecting to see no one that is sickly. The church is not a safe haven for the healed – it is a place where those needing healing come. While this chapter is not to discredit or excuse hurt that has taken place, especially while in the church, it is to bring light to an area not addressed and masked by obscurity with the truth, whether that is a truth we like or not.

On a more personal level, I have lived through the sting of being hurt while I was in the church as a lay member and in a leadership role in ministry. It is one of the places I have been ostracized and criticized, later realizing it was by hurt people, dissatisfied with themselves, lost, broken and dis-eased, in their frustration hurting others because they were not healed themselves. While another's healing is not my responsibility, in some respect it certainly became my burden until I chose to release it. One thing I learned in going through, is putting into perspective that I was hurt by imperfect people, not a perfect God nor the church He established. We must be careful that our selfishness does not make others accountable for our actions. Sadly, when people are hurt within the church the blame falls on the church as a whole (regardless of location) and is followed by a relationship with God plagued with distrust and stagnancy because they find it hard to recover and trust God again, though it was man who failed. *Can you relate to experiencing things in life that seemingly found you farther away from God the deeper you found yourself in the problem?* The will of God is never that you leave scarred and in worse condition than when you came but rather that you come, receive Him, learn, grow, change and compel others to come in.

When we come to the understanding of what it is that makes up the church we can see from a clearer point of view. The church is made up of everyday people, with regular problems who should be seeking change like the next person. There are several types of people that make up the attendance in the physical church; there are those who come to strengthen their relationship with God, those who come out of tradition and may be lacking or not understanding their relationship with God, those who believe by mouth but not by heart and those who do not know about God but are curious. It is important to know who and what you are dealing with in the church. Everyone, to be frank, does not have the same agenda. It is safe to say that everyone is not at church for God, although He is, or should be, the primary reason why, along with souls, the church fellowships together.

Without a proper understanding of what the church is and what the church does, negative occurrences are often misconstrued or labeled as the source of "church hurt". Honestly, with an understanding of the church, the same hurt can and has been experienced simply because of where it has taken place. How daunting of a reality it is to know that one can go to a hospital and acquire an infection or disease they didn't ask for or give permission to obtain. Hurt is a small word that occurs quickly and causes the greatest amount of damage, while forgiveness, the longer word, is harder to come by, and quicker to leave lest it be maintained. It is hard to forgive when the pains of the wound are sharp reminders of painful incidents and scars the remnants of what once took place. This is where we must seek *healing* — it is the one thing we all need but the process many forego because healing can, at times, hurt worse than the initial wound. In order to be healed, one must expose the wound and what caused it, communicate the signs and symptoms and go through stages of pain and discomfort before arriving at the "coveted" place.

Until we are healed, we will forever recount hurt & pain, rehearsing the way it made us feel and at times becoming complacent in a place that is not comfortable, walled in by pain, anger, sadness, pity, entitlement and an unwillingness to forgive. We hold on to forgiveness as a prized possession many are unworthy of while imprisoning ourselves by the deeds they have moved away from. Contrary to popular belief, forgiveness really is for you, not the one who has offended you; to offer forgiveness is to release the weight from you, the blame you carried that wasn't yours and to ultimately release the ball & chain of past events you've lugged around over time. We dress up by pretending we are okay, removing ourselves from the church, projecting that anger away from the offender and carrying it through life, taking it out on other situations and lugging the weight of times past along the way. Forgiveness is the product of necessary scary conversations, a dredging up of feelings that *"don't matter"*, a realization of sorries that may never be expressed and a release of tears, fears, and emotions suppressed that have been begging to come out.

Have you truly forgiven those that harmed you? Have you let go of the past and the things that have caused you to stray away? The enemy has a goal that you never let go of what has happened to you or brought you to where you are. If he can keep you in a place where you cannot bring yourself to come to the God of the church or forgive those that hurt you, he can also keep you in a place where you are out of the will of God and unable to receive forgiveness from Him for yourself. As long as the enemy can keep you trapped in the fear or refusal of facing and forgiving, he is not concerned about you moving on and growing up, because he is the puppet master controlling the strings. How long will you hold yourself back? Yes, they hurt you. No, they probably did not come back to rectify the situation. Yes, you deserve for them to make it right. Now, do you also deserve to move on and to live? Yes, you do! Don't give any person, place or thing so much power in your life that it costs you your peace. There are some things in life that we are entitled to that are not necessarily the best thing for us. While you have a right to be upset due to your experience, you also have a need to be free, at peace, and on the road to better.

Hebrews 12:14 – Follow peace with all men, and holiness, without which no man shall see the Lord.

Ephesians 5:27 – That He might present it to himself a glorious church, not having spot, or wrinkle, or any such thing; but that it should be holy and without blemish.

We must keep in mind that everyone that comes in and through the church has not received the gift of salvation *and* even those who have, will have issues to some extent because we all struggle along the way with emotions, human will, and battles of the flesh. It is not so much how we go through it, but how we GROW through it. Situations don't have to change you, but you should find change in it. What needs to be added or subtracted in you to equal the solution to be a better you? In understanding that the physical church is essentially the same yet a separate entity of the church we inhabit in our vessels, a greater understanding of church hurt ensues. The reason I say the physical church is a separate entity than the church we inhabit as spiritual beings are simple. The physical church is just a building; what makes it a church is those that come to gather there, the significance of the fellowship and of course the unified reverence of God in his deity. The spiritual church that we inhabit is one that we must maintain with prayer, worship, thanksgiving, compassion, and love towards others. If the physical church did not exist, that would not excuse the church within us from walking in what God has called us to do and being the salt of the earth and light in the world.

Matthew 5:13-14 Ye are the salt of the Earth: but if salt have lost his savor, wherewith shall it be salted? It is thenceforth good for nothing, but to be cast out, and to be trodden under the foot of men. 14 Ye are the light of the world. A city that is set on a hill cannot be hid.

Ephesians 5:8 – For ye were sometimes darkness, but now are ye light in the Lord: walk as children of the light.

We are all in the same boat. There are different positions in the Body of Christ, however, we are all in the same race striving for the same goal. At times we get to the church and our anticipation begins to exceed our need. Let's take a moment to be realistic. We get into the church expecting happy days and a carefree life, but forget about the work that must be done, the warfare that must be fought and the toiling of the ground to yield the harvest at hand. The truth is, at the point of accepting salvation we don't immediately encounter Heaven as we expect, but we begin the fight to escape Hell in a daily war in the Spiritual realm for our souls.

As the church, and leaders therein, we must always be in a position to meet the ever changing needs of the people, with the help of God, of course; people should, after all, come to church to be delivered and find a way out of their dire situations. The issue is not with the physical church, but rather those that come in. The church is not the place to find a comfort zone and be stagnant in life, but a place to learn, grow, and excel. The truth is that people may fail you, especially when you put them in a position to meet expectations they were never created for agreed to meet. Regardless of time in the church, titles held, positions walked in, and how much they seem to be together, people are still people who have issues and shortcomings. Hurt comes in more when a person that you expected more out of failed you in one way or another. Why do we place people on pedestals they never agreed to stand on, then get surprised when they fall and break themselves, the pedestal, and bruise us in the process coming down? We must cease to place unrealistic standards and expectations on people that were not built to meet them, and moreover, if we insist on doing so, be willing to meet and be measured by the same expectations we place upon others.

There is one perfect person and that is Jesus Christ Himself. We are to all, as we strive to walk in His image (Genesis

1:26), to pursue perfection, understanding that we attain true perfection when we die first to self and are, at some point, physically raptured to be with the Lord. Rightfully so, we will all be held accountable for our deeds and actions while upon this earth. Just as much as those who have hurt you will be held accountable, you have a mandate to fulfill the destiny for which you were created.

Romans 14:12 – So then every one of us shall give an account of himself to God.

Matthew 12:36 – But I say unto you, that every idle word that men shall speak, they shall give an account thereof in the day of judgment.

Fight the inner me, not the enemy

Do not allow yourself to be your greatest enemy. The battle with our "inner me" can be more damaging than the enemies we face, as we fight through misgivings, shortcomings, self-esteem, fear and doubt. Don't allow the challenges of your past to torment your growth today. If we allowed everything we went through to deter us from purpose, none of us would ever progress. The fact is that hurt is a part of the journey of our making; hurt / pain is the part of life I fully believe we would all forego if given the choice. Getting stuck on the hurt will have caused you to look up years later having progressed little in life past that point to where you should be. To walk in the image and ways of Jesus Christ, we must be prepared to do just that keeping in mind that the greatest source of "church hurt" was first experienced by Him. Jesus was crucified by the religious people... Not those with relationship but those who were practicing religion and tradition, while condemning in nature. He was damaged most, metaphorically of course, by the same people we face today, in a church that is not in them. Hurt is encountered on the path of life, but it is not the journey — it's just one of the necessary markers on the course of life. The greatest lessons are learned through what hurts us. Learn from it, visit is you must but do not move in and move on.

My thoughts on church hurt ...

Often, many tend to not have a full understanding of the repercussions of self-righteousness, self-exaltation and backbiting until they have experienced it themselves. While God will hold accountable in His own way those who have wronged, hurt and caused you to leave, you are equally accountable for your actions and failure to progress. I know it hurts, and it will not be easy, but can you seek God for yourself in spite of what they did or said? Will you be made whole or will you choose to wallow and hold yourself back from living a life of love, passion and purpose fulfilled? God never left you, forsook you, or abandoned you, even though at some points I am sure it felt as such. At some point, in spite of what they did, it doesn't excuse them but you must forgive. When you forgive truly, you open yourself to receive all that God has for you and His plan for your life.

The enemy, Satan, would prefer for you to hold on to what has hurt you and never step foot into the church building again; as an enemy of God he wants to be sure you stay as far away from God as possible to further validate his mission to discredit the Word of God and any positive association with it. I've learned that people will be people and the only one effective in changing them is God. You be the change you want others to see. We must let God be God. I can only speak to you as a living witness who sat dying at home and dead in the pews because I couldn't get past what "they" had done to me... I was slandered, ignored, made to cry many days, pushed, bruised, misused, and more... I had to decide to LIVE whether that meant using wisdom to confront some things and in others never get the closure deserved, while prioritizing my healing. Remember that no one in the church or person is perfect, even those with titles. We are all seeking and striving to get to know God better on a deeper level... we are all in need daily of forgiveness and deliverance and must seek such with a repentant heart. As much as we sometimes feel entitled to even place demands upon one's repentance or lack thereof, we are not God; Be more intentional about your healing and recovery than you are about their salvation, intentions and motives and you will see your path to healing much more clearly. At the end of it all, we are all sinners saved by grace, in need of a Savior.

Making Lo-debar work for you

Everybody is not equipped to carry you. Sometimes we rely too much and give people credit based off of what we have imagined or hoped for them to be. When you allow someone to carry you, who can hardly care for themselves your vulnerability leads to your susceptibility to fall. Often times we want to trust others because of their title, their charisma, the antics and perhaps the anointing on their life. The question remains, "Do you really know them or are you enamored with the thought of what they represent?"

In the Book of 2 Samuel 4, the story of Mephibosheth **[muh-fib-uh-sheth]** is found. A child who has just lost the foundation of his Father Jonathan and Grandfather Saul to death, too vulnerable to fight for his own life and too naïve to understand the times, finds himself being carried in haste to avoid the possibility of suffering the same fate. The nurse carrying him was running to save his life and that of her own. Along the way after encountering an unknown obstacle she trips and unintentionally drops him, causing Mephibosheth foo all in such a way that he is immediately gravely injured and deemed crippled. Although Mephibosheth was not intentionally dropped, he was dropped and injured nonetheless, a clear indicator that it takes more than willingness to carry another, more so spiritually than physically.

The hurt he experienced at the hands of one not equipped to carry him caused him, as time went on, to go to a low place in his mind, heart, and spirit on the road to giving up. He lived in a place called Lo-debar which literally means "no words", "no communication", decrepit and desolate of life, a place of darkness, wilderness and depression. Mephibosheth seems to have not much going for him. His name means "despised one", he's now physically impaired, he has no friends or family remaining that is spoken of and no place to go. Mephibosheth decides he will reside in Lo-debar and ultimately die there. More than just a geographical location, metaphorically Lo-debar was a place of defeat without the aesthetics; combine the surroundings with a state of mental defeat, physical defeat, & a destitute spirit and you have a recipe lethal dose of helplessness! What we must understand is we will all get to places in life that we don't particularly like or understand; The beauty of it just being a place means you have every right to leave or to stay.

Mephibosheth had come to a point where he has lost his will to live a meaningful life and gives in to the natural state of his situation of hopelessness. We must fight the fight of faith even when faith is all we have so that our circumstances don't become a defining factor in our lives. Our spiritual walk and the trials we go through were never guaranteed to be easy but we have an advocate in Jesus Christ and Father who won't forsake us, loves us unconditionally, and carries us with his grace and mercy. You may feel defeated and appear to be in a situation of hopelessness but your victory is really as simple as your perspective. If you see yourself defeated you will be. Your Lo-debar may never be a physical place but it may be depression, that dead-end relationship, finances, a decision gone wrong, or even your walk with God. Whatever situation you are in is never HOPELESS - turn your faith up to the highest setting and walk with your head held high, only looking down momentarily to see where you are going.

1 Corinthians 13:13 – And now these three remain: faith, hope, and love and the greatest of these is love.

The word "remain" is to continue, abide, and is applied to persons remaining in a place, in a state or condition, in contradistinction from removing or changing their place, or passing away. Here, to remain must be understood to be used to denote "permanency," when the other things of which he had spoken had passed away; and the sense is, that faith, hope, and love would "remain" that is, these should survive them all. Choose to see your Lo-debar through the eyes of faith, hope and love and watch things change for you. Current tribulations and situations do not have to become a permanent residence. Serve an eviction notice on the Lo-debars of your life and LIVE! We cannot become prideful and allow ourselves to forget that God has saved many of us in our lowest place. Often times, we don't take God to the deep, dark, deserted areas of our lives for shame and feeling as if we have failed him; these are the times God can work the best in us and through us. The longer we try to figure out a situation that only divine intervention can resolve, the longer we will remain in our desolate places in life.

Many years after living in Lo-debar divine intervention

changed the life of a now adult Mephibosheth. King David, who was once a childhood friend of Jonathan, the now deceased father of Mephibosheth, inquired many years later about any possibility of survivors from the lineage of Saul / Jonathan due to their brotherhood. Upon finding out that Jonathan's son was alive, he summoned for him in an effort to show kindness to any survivor of his fallen friend & brother. Mephibosheth, thinking he would die, felt even more helpless and had resolved that he had met his end. Why? Fear had once again illegally crept in and invaded his moment to recover and move forward in his mind.

When Mephibosheth arrived at the palace, David not only showed him kindness, but continually dined with him at the King's table, showered him with the finest of garments / gifts and favored him! Mephibosheth literally went from destitute to destiny! His defeat became THEE feat he had longed for all of his life... Why? Because of a blood covenant David made with Jonathan, his Father! What am I saying? Your situation has no choice but to turn around because of the blood covenant with the Father! The sooner you believe and pursue the forgiveness, freedom, and fearlessness that belongs to you, the closer to the horizon you shall be. Mephibosheth's life is a testament that even in the lowest of places and after time has elapsed and you feel forgotten, someone knows where you are! God, at the appointed time, can and will meet you where you are at and cause men to summons you to greener pastures.

If you never get it right with them, get it right with you

and for you. Your life, happiness, healing, and deliverance depend on your breakthrough. You cannot afford to be entrapped by the actions of others. Let God deal with everything and everyone associated with your pain and at the same time allow him to deal with you. You can't be the judge and the jury. Your hurt didn't break you because you have made it to today... Your hurt didn't kill you because it wasn't your time to go. Allow what has wounded you to be the very thing that propels you to be great! Allow your disappointments and your pain to be stepping stones to your destiny. You are the people in the church. The church is in you. We are the church. Be careful to represent the church the way God intended and as hard as it may be pray for those that do otherwise. Don't allow anyone or anything to stand in the way of your freedom.

In my situation, I have had some people come back and repent and others not at all; when they did return they found me living. Some people know what they did and because of the shame they may not have enough courage to come to you, feeling that they deserve the rejection they presume they would get from you as a result of the pain they caused, and are too prideful to accept any other scenario. Remember that a person who has not forgiven themselves will not know how to seek forgiveness from someone else. Is the person who has offended you deceased? Forgive them too! Find the avenue that you must travel to find healing through counseling, therapy, coaching, writing letters, etc,. Forgive. Love anyway. Seek God in spite of. The church didn't hurt you, they did. Now allow the church to be the church and be healed. I know this is a touchy subject for some, but healing is so necessary to get where God needs us to go!

We cannot associate the imperfect actions of others with a perfect God. Once we become the church we were called to be and allow the church to be the church in the physical building, it is my belief that church hurt won't be prevalent.

Forgive often. Love more. Learn Daily.

3

Failure to Launch

The Vision

Nothing can be effectively accomplished without a blue-print or a plan. Ideas are birth in the mind after original inspiration by God, to be carried out by us, the individual. When we are given a vision it is either to help someone else build or to build on our own, both for a greater good. The vision will often manifest through dreams, written thoughts, planning, and ultimately purposeful execution. The gifts and callings that God has graced us with are all a part of the greater vision for our lives. It is our job to follow through, seek God, and launch.

Too many people sit in and out of the church dying because they have failed to work the vision. God does not grace us with dreams, gifts, callings, visions, and help to carry out without a greater purpose in mind. What has God given you that is going without use? What gifts has God graced you with that are lying dormant? What vision has God given you and equipped you to accomplish that is dying day by day? Distraction is the archenemy to destiny as procrastination is to progression. Often times we say we are moving forward, or attempting to do so, but are held back; whether hindered on your own accord or due to the actions of others, the choice to progress belongs to you. Are they really holding you back or are you your biggest obstacle?

When God gives you the vision, he equips you to carry it out to completion. Along the same lines He also gives you strength for the journey and the ability to adapt along the way; He removes the things we don't need while adding what we do to make the blueprint come to fruition according to His purpose and plan. We must get into a place where we trust the plan enough to walk by faith into the vision. Anything and everything that we do for God we must do with all of our might and all of our strength, with the understanding that doing it for God is doing it for His people and His Kingdom that HE alone would get the glory!

God-given revelation, does not excuse us from doing the work required to bring the manifestation to pass. If the seed has been given to you, the responsibility of nurturing, growing and birthing the harvest of that vision falls upon your shoulders. This relates to being "Dead in the Pews" because so many sit on what has given to them watching the world go by, and ending up bitter because they never made the choice to walk in the ability God gave them to make changes in the world. How many do you know who sit next to you Sunday after Sunday, and weekday after weekday, a shell of the person they once were, living beneath their potential, merely existing? Do you personally have the zeal you once had? Do you feel an overwhelming need to fulfill purpose in life? These are questions we must ask ourselves and be willing to face our answers realistically, no matter the response.

Often times we put too much energy into what we were given, but less into the effort, time, talent, and treasure to see it to execution. Having a plan is not one and the same with the determination it takes to help it evolve into a tangible product. Walking purposefully does not stop at the vision. What benefit is a beautifully wrapped gift that you never open and put to use? Such is vision. When you are inspired to do something great, it is imperative to write the vision, plan to execute, and do what it takes to see it in action. *Jeremiah 29:11 reminds us that "before we were in the womb God knew us" (Paraphrase),* meaning God knew who or what we would be, what destiny would be assigned to you, our shortcomings, our successes, and everything in between.

An architect is not just as good as his blueprint, but more so the creative ability to make what is at once just a sketch come to life. Without the architect the constructor has nothing to build; without construction there is no venue to hold the vision of others and create a space for them to create and re-cycle the visionary process. Be the architect of your vision, knowing that what you create or are destined to do

/ be is not just for you; someone else's destiny may depend upon your launch. God doesn't impregnate our being with ideas to become overwhelmed by the dust of our unproductive mind. That thought must become real enough to us to be handled, tangible, and full of promise to be birth and positioned to help someone else. From the outside a seed looks plain, without promise and ultimately a candidate for disposal. In a seed, the potential of what is to come is masked by obscurity, while it is exposed to everything that could destroy it until the appointed time to come forth, bloom, and show the world what it was created to be all along. Many will take you for granted based on what they see, but never forget that you are a promise!

The Runway

Behind every great flight of success there is a background. A flight is not most successful because it is in the air, but rather made by what it took to get off the ground and what it takes to safely land. If you think about it, staying in the air is easy if it's based solely on maintaining balance, discerning one's surroundings, and avoiding obstacles that could end the flight and endanger those who have trusted us to come aboard our vision.

An airplane will never successfully fly without a runway. There are things that take place on the runway that happen nowhere else; without the humbling place there will be many false starts, crash landings, and potential fatalities. Why? A plane that has not prepared for the flight, and conditioned the engine, is not ready to fly. There is a process prior to flying that no one can do for you; skipping steps and skimming corners is always evident in the end product. Often when we hear about plane crashes / mishaps, it's a misjudged mechanical issue, a failure to stop to assess when problematic situations arise and, at times, due to inexperience or flying on the wrong radar, disappearing all together never to be located again.

A plane is intricately built to do one thing — fly; you were created to do one thing — purpose. The airplane was not invented just to hold people or sit on a shiny display, but rather to carry great weights, withstand insurmountable pressure and move. Those who build the plane intentionally put it through a battery of repetitive difficult tests to ensure it will be able to survive regardless of what situations it encounters. We are built in such a way that every time we weather a storm, we are enabled with the tools to resist, endure, and ultimately conquer. Think about the times in life when we have avoided the runway; now skip forward mentally to the end result. The trial and error is needed at times to avoid the heartache that was unnecessarily experienced due to our own gullibility. Your runway experience is mandatory to qualify you for the journey ahead.

Let's dissect what takes place between the plane and the runway before the launch:

Visual Analysis: The airplane is visually inspected for any character flaws, obvious defects and of course any derivations from the original design to be sure the vision LOOKS the part. Thought it's not all about the appearance, the fact is a vision must be seen in an appealing light; a vision that has manifested tangibly is a direct reflection on the inventor / creator.

We can't get so caught up in looking the part that we have no action to back up our appearance. It is, however, necessary that we allow ourselves to go through the process of grooming, changing and growing as we evolve into the vision which is a testament to the ability of God to change the unchangeable and do wonders with the impossible. I believe we have all been to a point in life where change seems out of our reach. We live in a society stuck on "come as you are" and "God knows my heart" while scarce are those that are open and available to be vessels meet for the Master's use.

Inspection: The diagnostic check is a very vital part of the runway process. During this time, someone who knows the intricate working of the plane details, construction, and functions checks to be sure all is in place. The diagnostic check creates tests and trials on the equipment to stress it to a point where it will show any flaws if currently present which would denote the need for necessary delay and repair. Anything out of place and malfunctioning is immediately flagged and flight will not be permitted until clearance is given by the Inspector.

This is how our lives should be in our relationship with

God. Frequent diagnostic checks are imperative for a successful flight. One should not be determined to take off in a state of desperation, especially when the Inspector has found a need for repair or delay to make things right. Any good manufacturer is concerned about the inspection — it is perhaps one step that will never get old. Why? The manufacturer has tirelessly worked on their creation, toiling in the mind, sketching it out and even taking time to form it to perfection with their own hands. In an obsessive way, the manufacturer always wants to be assured that every part is in order, every function properly operating and every facet is just as it was originally envisioned to be. God is not a manufacturer, but by nature he is a creator; a manufacturer creates from things that already exist and makes something awesome; a creator takes nothing and makes something great often never to be duplicated. You were not manufactured, you were created! A true creator will always stand by their work with unconditional love even when it seems to be a failure in the eyes of others. How powerful is His love for us that at our weakest point when we cannot fly he nurses us back and loves us through it all?

Topping off: As the diagnostic check determines that all parts are operationally functional, the time is taken to add components to heighten performance.

The radar (discernment) is checked to ensure the connection with the controller at all times, lest an invader sneak in and invade the space destined for that plane at that time. Be mindful of who, what, when, where, and why. Know what is in your space at all times. As the pilot must keep in contact with the controller, a prayer life is a necessity to know when a change in your immediate atmosphere has taken place, or when a sudden shift is necessary.

Oil is added to ensure the engine has the capability to rotate, move, and function well without unnecessary friction which causes overheating. The oil (anointing) is not just a protector but it's also a lubricant that renders the vessel effective. Trying to operate machinery without the correct amount of oil or with a substitute will lead to irreparable damage to the parts and at times a total burn out or explosion that cannot be reversed resulting in unnecessary casualties of war

.

Fuel is dispensed to enable the plane to get where it needs to go. The fuel (Holy Ghost) not only allots the plane the power to go, but also the assurance to protect it in case of an accidental landing, an emergent situation or to move further than the intended destination until the next "filling." You can have a perfect plane in vision, have passed the checks initially, and have fluids but without fuel you will only go so far if anywhere at all. The interesting thing about a motor is you can try and trick it with another substance but it recognizes a smokescreen and will not budge. The Holy Spirit is necessary and cannot be substituted!

Loading of cargo is important as what you carry affects how you fly. It is never recommended that you choose to transport hazardous chemicals as it is detrimental to you as well as anything else you have on board. One must be mindful not to compromise their cargo by way of contamination just to boast of having something on board. Surround yourself with those you can trust to complete thorough security checks so while you are in the inspection process, they are ensuring nothing will come aboard to compromise your destiny by endangering the plane. Only carry the baggage checked, weighed and approved for the journey; stowaways, additional weight and unauthorized contents can cause excessive cost, reroutes and delayed arrival to your final destination.

Momentum is gained by trial error. The runway is long lengthwise to give the plane an opportunity to build up speed all while enduring drag and pull from the winds and elements and pressure from the surroundings. As momentum increases power is gained from the forces that, to others, may appear to slow you down. Without everything that comes against it the plane would not be tenacious enough to build up enough courage and speed to take off. Thus, every trial, temptation, and test survived were all necessary drag and pull to build the pressure to withstand and succeed in your life.

The launch

So often, we have an unrealistic expectation of what the launch really is and how we go about "making it happen." Yes, we only have so much control, however, using what we do have can only be one of two things: powerful or disastrous.

We are empowered to dream, create, possess, own, mandate, decree, and declare! With all of the knowledge we have and hopes we hold on to, how do we fail to launch? We tend to forget that we are the plane, those aboard are the vision, and flight is our destiny. Whatever it takes to fly is our responsibility.

Faith is undoubtedly a necessary component to launch. In fact, launching without faith is planning to fail. When God gives you a vision that puzzle piece belongs to you; where / how you fit it and find its purposed place depends upon the journey you choose to take. He may give other people similar assignments, as we all have a common goal, but no one person can do what you were called to do, except you. Out of all the planes out on the tarmac they all have different times, destinations, cargo to carry and times to be there, though the end result will be the same. Due to the fact that your destiny belongs to you, it is not the fault of any other one person when you don't "takeoff" as planned.

There are many factors to consider in the takeoff outside of the mechanical checks. Timing is everything! While the destination may be clear and all of the internal or external checks have been passed you must not take off until the set time to avoid crashes in the spiritual realm. There are four factors that are essential to success journeys: servanthood, submission, accountability, and responsibility. A quote by an unknown person once said that if 'serving is above you, leading is beyond you. One must be submitted to God first and leadership; you cannot lead well being a poor follower; however, one that follows well will be an effective leader. Leading is best done by example, not pointing the way, but rather showing how it is done. If you, by chance, do not have a local person you are submitted to, things must be done decently and in order regardless of the reporting structure. It is important to know that everyone should have someone to hold them accountable and keep them balanced or level-headed; even Jesus had God.

Failure to takeoff due to someone holding you back will never be an acceptable excuse. An effective leader who is especially discerning will groom you with the help of God to reach your destined place. Be prayerful about the places you submit yourself to, as all ground is simply not good ground. If you have a leader that is pouring into you and providing an atmosphere conducive to growth glean as much as you can to prepare for the tasks at hand. You must also be open to correction and guidance, which is where submission sometimes comes in. Can you stand to be corrected when it is for your good? The tools needed to be effective are gained through listening, following, learning and communicating. If your leader is in tune with God and you are remaining prayerful the time to launch will present itself. One thing about takeoff is you will never have to force it; at some point enough momentum is gained that the plane lifts off the runway at the appointed time when the gear is in the right hands.

While on the subject of the leadership, submission is key, however, it is equally important for YOU to know who you were called to be and what you were called to do. A leader can give you the tools but no one can make you use them. Sitting on the gifts that you are given waiting for a golden ticket or awe-inspiring opportunity runs the risk of waiting for a moment that may never happen thus leaving you miserable with a destiny unfulfilled. Earlier the question was presented concerning those who are a shell of the person they once were. What causes this phenomenon? Lack of purpose. You see, anything that is not living up to its ability just exists. How many people do you see on the pews of life that have the potential to be world changers? Just as God sees us, we often see more in others than they see in themselves. On a daily basis we are surrounded by those with great gifts, lost, existing waiting for someone to speak a word or breath life on their tired bones that have grown weary from barely existing. Some don't fail to launch because they know what they are supposed to do and refuse to move; still others do not know and have not sought God, while many more fail to launch because they will not submit to what was chosen for them against their personal will.

Most importantly, promotion comes from God, not man. Often times we get enamored with the person and somehow God gets placed on the back burner. While this is not always intentional, our distraction that causes us to forget to keep God first can place us in an awkward position. Where the course veers off is idolatry, the act of placing complete trust, will, hope or belief in a person, place, or thing absent of God. We can idolize ourselves or those around us, most certainly to our detriment. Yes, you can trust to a fault! Misplaced worship, honor, and glory will always in some way, shape, or form lead to disappointment. Do not put so much of your hope in man and where they can take you that you take the God who has created, called, and entrusted you for granted.

You were destined to takeoff. Launching is in your destiny. There is no perfect moment, timing, announcement or parade. You must trust God enough to do what you were created for. Existing will get you nowhere fast, while living will take you everywhere you are purposed to be. Not just living as in waking daily, but living in Christ, seeking God for plans, believing His promises, and moving by no less than great faith. You must believe in you. Even if all the people in the world believe in you and your God-given abilities, you must get to a point where you believe enough to birth it to manifestation. What you believe you will follow and what you follow you will emulate, reproduce, & bring to pass.

Eulogize doubt, bury fear and face your destiny head on!

4

Acquired Immunity

The natural tendency of the human being to adapt to our environment can be disadvantageous in the less than ideal situation. While not all environments are bad, even the best of situations is not a direct indicator that one is in the right place. Making the choice to be in some places in life are likened to being in an atmosphere surrounded by contagions, attacked by the invisible force of infectious disease. We are most vulnerable at our most unsuspecting moments rendering us a target of acquired immunity by way of cross contamination.

Acquired immunity takes place when the body, mind, and even spirit are continually exposed to contamination that eventually invade, reside, and cause the vessel to lose the ability to fight off foreign material. Immunity transpires when resistance is low and defenselessness is high, tricking the vessel into accepting what has come to invade as a welcome party. Cross- contamination ensues when, through our naivety, and at times, choice, we place our roots in dominant territory having no choice but to submit to the seed already there; the resulting byproduct is one that appears to be unsure of its original purpose and equally lost as to where it will culminate. Things that come to occupy your being and attempt to force you off course can come in the form of people, places, things, and spirits. Often times, initially, you will find yourself fighting to do what's right with defense mechanisms in place with hopes of staying on the right path; it is after repeated attempts, each time leaving a deposit in the host environment, that the vector takes up residence to live, grow, multiply and ultimately take over. It is surmised that in this fragile state one's need to feel wanted, needed, and accepted find themselves losing control of their inhibitions.

People

Everybody has an innate desire to be loved, fulfilling every meaning of the word, and that, unconditionally. Our need for acceptance when confronted with past hurts and pains like abandonment, neglect, and loneliness can propel us into the paths of people who sense our need but lack the capacity to satisfy it. The aura that we radiate is often telling of the paths and people we choose, either falling into the way of those who can gratify or those who cannot, that portray the ability to complete us in ways that leave us at our emptiest point. Often, people become our crutch because they are our enablers, at which point acceptance isn't about them, but solely about another finding a place to be everything they have fought to face. Who we choose to expose ourselves to tend to be our balanced reflection; the mirror behind the smokescreen.

People become our crutch when we find the place where it is not just safe to be ourselves, but, a haven away from righteous judgement; the word we are all scared to say and indignant to face for fear it may be the change we require. When you find yourself in a state of self-destruction in any sense of the word the last thing you want is to be exposed. Self-destruction, while it sounds abhorrent, is any act that is morally, civilly, or even emotionally incorrect that causes you to do anything against the natural physical, mental, emotional and social needs of your being. There are two things that will cause us to self-destruct: our adaptation to and environment that is conducive to said behavior or our desire to cover up our innate needs with pseudo satisfaction to avoid facing who or what we really are. Have you made every attempt to be who you were created to be? Many of us have not submitted to our created being, because who we were created to be doesn't fit the mold of who we want to be; this will cause us to go in a downward cycle against the law of nature in an attempt to find ourselves on a lost journey.

We have all heard the clichés that come with those we choose to surround ourselves with:

"Birds of a feather flock together"
"You are who you hang around"

"When you sleep with dogs, you will get up with fleas"

The reality is, when you find yourself in a situation with a person you know is not healthy or *destined* for you, there is a great chance you have found your stability in an injurious presentation. How? Some people represent the place one can go to do anything they feel is right without the prerequisite of being judged and made to feel less than. The truth is judgment doesn't come to make you feel low or less but to show you the opportunity to do better, be more, and make better decisions. Judgement, in the right hands, is an expression of conviction wrapped in love, truth, restoration and access to the tools to build a bridge over your offenses leading to a pathway to righteousness. Judgement absent agape love is another wound to the soul and offense to the spirit. The person that is right for you, be it a friend, associate, loved one or significant other will never take you on a path to continue self-destruction. God will never give you someone or something that will take you farther out of His will.

The people you choose to be around should better you as you better them. The unspoken rule is to find yourself with those that are above where you are and further along than you are in life. Being around those that are on the path to better gives you access to tools and insight to leave where you are and get where you are needed. You cannot be successful until you are present in your purposed state. People who will enable you to continue on a path to not be purposed are not just dangerous to you, but are using you to enable them as well. As you find no need to push greater out of one another you find yourself being accepted in a state of mind you once never imagined you'd be or had fought against becoming; more so, the person on the opposite end has found an avenue to continue on the dead end they have uneventfully traveled without reason to better themselves as they are acknowledged and empowered as they are. Don't find yourself weak and vulnerable, affected by every blow of the wind, and infected by the negative environments your needs have created. It's one thing to be contagious, however, it's another altogether to be susceptible and polluted by those you have trusted to protect you in your time of need.

So, what do you do when you find yourself drawn to the very thing that you know is bad for you, but somehow you can't get away? There are different reasons why you feel like you cannot simply cut the ties and walk away.

Familiar spirits – We can find ourselves drawn to people more on a subconscious or spiritual level because beneath the surface they embody secrets, struggles, temptations, intentions and a darkness that on some level we knowingly or unknowingly identify with. Familiar spirits is stronger than our flesh so we can find ourselves enticed by someone that we may know deep down is not for us, but at the same time is an addiction that we cannot break and a bad habit that we subconsciously crave; when familiar spirits attract and attach the person is a danger to you that you view as a safe place and its hard to cut that tie. This is not a connection that scissors can cut and you move on, but one that can only be broken by intentional movement and action, prayer, fasting as led, and feeding your spirit through the Word of God (the right spirit) to counteract the fleshly desire the person may represent. When you don't move past a tie, especially when you have come to the realization that their time is up, you may begin to harbor resentment, exhibit anger and experience mental and physical sickness. Why, you mask ask? Because familiar spirits go deeper than you. Familiar spirits know what it takes to draw you, entice you and keep you and different acts such as pacts, covenants, sexual contact, etc., deepens the tie.

As humans we know what we want, we pursue it, and seemingly think we know it all and have everything under control, but the reality is when it comes to the things of the spirit, we are dumb if not for God and His guidance! We must know and come to terms with the fact that this flesh is not good and that we all have things to deal with; it is imperative to ask God to reveal to you the areas you do not know are there, the things you ignore or choose not to deal with, and to bring to surface every selfish intent and desire that separates you from Him so that those things can be dealt with and you can be delivered and freed.

Fear – A person can represent a safe place from everything you are subconsciously afraid of while simultaneously becoming the prison of the manifestation of the covered, hidden, wounds of the past that remain not healed. Chapter 7 will deal with fear on a deeper level.

Places

Places, whether geographically or mentally, can trap us if we so allow. At times, being in certain locations enable us to escape our truth while others become our new reality with the daunting prospect of permanence becoming all too real, the longer we choose to stay. No, every place is not wrong. The caveat is moving away or going on when you know you are not in the right place. What is the right place? While not necessarily geographical, the right place will teach you, provide opportunities for growth — should you see and take advantage of them — and most importantly, allow destiny and purpose to flow in the right timing. You can be in a place that is the right "type" of place that still does not qualify it to be your destined locale — there are great homes, churches, places of employment, etc., everywhere, but they do not all have your destiny in their blueprint. Purpose must always be a top priority.

We can become immune to an environment simply because of the comfort level being there provides. As human beings we often settle where our emotions find a home; if we FEEL safe / secure, welcomed, needed, wanted, desired, etc., we label that place as home. Every place that feels like home is not meant for you to reside. Any place that hinders your growth or disables your ability to be better is a breeding ground for acquired immunity as it relates to complacency, convenience and conformity. Habitual settling when you are meant to excel leads to chronic complacency. Dreams are not turned into realities by sleeping while the world passes by. Dreams are shown to you while sleeping to give you the tools to act and bring manifestation to them when you are awake. There is too much destiny in you to settle!

Things

We all have our things that we hold on to; our security blankets of sorts to give us reassurance that we are doing something like the right thing. How often we find security in our homes, careers, money, cars, possessions, and fears. Yes, fears. We hold on to our entitlement to possess what we have obtained and fear that letting go will leave us without something to fall back on. Take a moment to think about one thing you are afraid to lose and why. If it were to disappear tomorrow, could you go on?

It may sound odd for one to find security in fear, but it is possible. I, for years, found security in all of my fears because they didn't require much of me; the fear of failing, the fear of succeeding, the fear of being judged, ridiculed, hurt, abandoned... the list goes on and on. I was so bound by those fears that I built a fortress with them and hid behind it, convinced that if I never came out, I wouldn't have to face the what-ifs on the other side. Fear can be paralyzing, stunting your growth and ultimately deterring you from your destiny. Like fear, the other things we hold on to become our crutch — our reason to remain handicapped or our excuse not to step out on faith. Fear has a way of making us feel entitled to have misgivings, so much so we become invulnerable to fear and disguise it as necessary precaution. We must get to a point that regardless of how daunting the outcome looks we move by faith; if we never take a chance, we'll seldom know what success looks like.

The security of our possessions and the success we have obtained with things that are fleeting must be curbed. As market values change, what we once considered success could very well end up being our downfall or disappointment. Success is less about what you have obtained and more about what you invest in that continually yields a return. Investing in dreams, destiny, education, and goals are wise investments that not only yield a return but also offer opportunity to grow, expand, and create assets. Trusting in possessions that depreciate as soon as the bow is removed will only later lead to a recycling of continual purchases of more items to depreciate to replace the last. While it is okay to purchase items and enjoy the finer things in life, we must remember, success is not measured by what you own but rather what you operate.

Being delivered from acquired immunity

To be delivered literally means to cut loose or be set free. Commonly, when a person is resistant to something, it is a lifetime of invulnerability, as the body / mind has literally changed to adapt to its familiar surroundings. As beings who are ever changing and growing we have the great opportunity afforded to use to break the chains of immunity if we so choose. How? By submitting our will to God's with the determination to move forward in His plans for our lives, we can live again! It is my belief that rarely does a person particularly choose to be bound, unsuccessful or trapped by fear in life. No one has ever said being called by God is easy; we are generally entrapped by fear of failing at something we never saw ourselves equipped with the capacity to be. While God may have chosen you to be something you never envisioned, you cannot play creator and do everything it takes to avoid your purpose coming to pass or your necessity for being upon the earth slowly diminishes. Think of it this way — a car was meant to drive and nothing else. If it no longer serves its purpose it is eventually towed, scrapped, crushed, and repurposed as something else IF there is anything left. Are you meeting your purpose or are you moving up on the tow list?

In order to change immunity the only options are to remain medicated indefinitely or change your environment. Change is inevitable, but growth is optional. Reality can be a hard thing to face; of all the things we confront in life, we are the most difficult to contain. As we segue into the next chapter, we have to do just that. We've talked about fear, now let us prepare to confront it.

5

Identity Crisis

HELP! I don't know who I am. I have no clue what I am supposed to be. I don't have any ideas as to how to get to my destiny. I am unsure where I belong. When will I know THE time is the right time? The questions never cease, and the reservations invade our steps with a vengeance matched wit for wit by our doubt. These are all questions that have plagued us all at some point in time. This undoubted insecurity is what makes you human. Your inability to figure it all out qualifies you to be a mere mortal; not expected to figure it out, know it all, or have it all together. We weren't created to know it all, but to BE all we were created to be. It's hard to be when you are not sure what that is.

We live in a society now where anything goes. Sexual identity is marred by same sex unions, transgender lifestyles, sex change operations, freedom of sexuality and casual sex is the new face, in some instances, of a committed relationship that may or may not end in the ordinance of God called marriage. Men are not confident in being men and women feel more welcome emulating a man by appearance, demeanor, personification and emasculating those they are "threatened by" or the person who comes along to challenge their independence. Still more are in the middle being a little bit of both because the prospect of having to choose is daunting, overshadowed by a lack of confidence and a need to feel accepted. Traditional marriage is slowly becoming old-fashioned and common-law rates are at an all-time high competing for what our new normal shall become. Suicide is now considered an honorable way to die by some, and murder is running rampant in the streets, none of which is discriminating by age, race, time, or place.

People are dying every day to hopes, dreams, and aspirations finding little reason to try again to succeed. Still others are thirsting for the limelight that heightens imperfections, just to be known, when in fact they don't know themselves at all. How did we get here? We are a people, a nation, generation after generation, who know of God but have lost our reverence; we have replaced fear where hope once lived, and masked our insecurities or ignorance by anything that goes. We are a society that is lost; tricked by the enemy to believe that this normal is the way it always should have been masked by his enmity with God and agenda to discredit anything related to the Word of God. What we see unfolding are the results of people who do not know who they are, but have an idea of what they have chosen to be according to personal will.

We are living in the midst of a generation and people who value the title above the work and the qualification of the call. Hebrews 13:21 & Philippians 1:6 expound on the fact that when God calls us he simultaneously equips us for the work and for the building of the Body of Christ. Nowadays, the title to do the work, absent the skill and anointing to be effective, can be bought online for a nominal fee, handed out like candy by someone even less qualified, or thrown around as novelties amongst the brethren absent the reverence of the call and the respect of many of a sacred office / gift. This will step on toes, but the same truth that hurts and cuts will also set us free. Ephesians 4:1 is a part of the letter to the church from Paul urging us from him, as a prisoner of Christ, "to walk worthy of the vocation wherewith we are called." The term prisoner is not indicative of one in bondage but rather one under the authority of another, submitted to their will and understanding that all that they seek to accomplish is not for self-gain but for the glory of a greater good. Walking worthy must be connotative of the labor and the fruit produced as a result of, not what you are called while doing it. This is significant because while we have many notable, significant vessels in the gospel, we have just as many prancing around for a name and doing no work; more so, we have those stagnant and sitting in the pews not working because society has coined them less than significant because of the lack of a prefix on their name or an automatic disqualification because of what they been or are going through. The challenge is to walk in obedience and ensure that there is no vainglory and everything you need to accomplish the work shall be provided.

A part of knowing who we are in Christ means that we must know and keep our assigned place. We are in a time now especially where it seems so many are hungry for the spotlight or attention, but few are willing to stay behind the scenes to develop, glean, and master the role for which they have been called. A good understudy will work to become skilled in the starring role, perfecting the lines and becoming the part, while never stepping on the toes of the holder of the placeholder of the featured character / person. Because we have so many stars now in the Gospel and not as many "understudies" we are in an era where Jesus is overshadowed, in some instances, by the grandeur, fame, fan clubs, and limelight of the ministry that is supposed to highlight his work upon the Earth and his sacrifice upon the cross. True ministry highlights the work of Jesus on the cross and His sacrifice upon the cross and the works of God to bring glory to the Kingdom of God, not to push us as vessels into the spotlight we are not worthy of. As the understudy masters their role, we are to study holiness and the attributes of God to emulate Him and walk in His image, not take the lead.

Though we have those who operate with the spirit of discernment, prophecy and even those who are used by God to reveal the unknown to us, the one person or being who should be able to tell us WHO we are is God. Why? In Jeremiah 1:5 there is a dialogue of sorts between God and Jeremiah when Jeremiah is doubtful of the call of God on His life for various reasons and God informs Him that *"He knew him before he was formed in his Mother's womb."* God knows us before our parents can formulate the thought to have a child, therefore, the call or the assignment is assigned to the seed pre-conception, destiny is a forethought, and our lives a blueprint and piece of the master plan for the glory to be revealed. Because God knows us intimately, especially so because He made us, He doesn't make mistakes when He calls us. He knows our faults, shortcomings, what we will do, won't do, and the path we will take to get there; what's amazing is He chooses us anyway. Intermingled with his will for our lives is our self-will where only we can determine if we choose the path of obedience and accomplish what we are destined to do or take the chance of self-gratification in an effort to find ourselves.

Know God, Know you

How can we know who we are if we do not know who God is? I submit to you that we cannot. We have seen and heard countless stories of those who were abandoned at birth, put up for adoption or are products of broken homes or parents who passed away that never fully find themselves until they know where they have come from; this inability to connect the pieces of the puzzle have left many wondering where they belong and worried if they fit at all. God is related to us as individuals, because though our parents were chosen to conceive us and we physically look like them, our spiritual DNA comes from our creator, not our natural parents. The

DNA we get from God is made up of His character, attributes, and the fruit of the spirit. In order to know who we are we must search to understand who He is to find ourselves in Him.

We have too many operating for God without relationship with Him which is a dangerous place to be. You cannot effectively represent someone you do not know or understand. How can you tell the guise under which one operates without assuming? By their works, the fruit they bare and the motive behind which they labor. To operate for God, absent relationship, is the equivalent to a ship without sails and a car without a wheel, traveling haphazardly until the inevitable crash happens endangering the operator, those on the bandwagon, and those in their path. Some operate for works, others for recognition of self, and still others generational tradition / lineage and monetary gain. We are reminded that absent of God none of this will matter by way of the scripture found in 2 Corinthians 5:9-10:

"So we make it our goal to please Him, whether we are at home in the body or away from it. For we must all appear before the judgment seat of Christ, so that each of us may receive what is due us for the things done in the body, whether good or bad."

The message in this verse reminds us that our focus is to remain on pleasing God, not people or ourselves for that matter because there is no eternal value in anything outside of the will of God for our lives. Hence, the weighted saying, 'only what we do for Christ will last.'

How can we get to know God on a deeper level, other than the "God" we encounter at church or through the preached messages? Relationship. Building an effective relationship takes time, attention, unity, honesty, communication, trust, vision, love, hope, compromise, and reciprocation. The same effort we have put into our natural relationships are just as beneficial to our relationship with God. In order to build with Him, we must have a firm foundation grounded upon these principles. As we open ourselves to Him and His will our needs are inevitably met as the law of reciprocation is birth out of what we wholly give to one both worthy of our gifts and able to give to our capacity to receive. Each principle is vital to our relationship in the following ways:

Time is a principle that is two-fold with God who both grants time and *is* time. In our society today we not only tend to take what we are allotted for granted, but we also in the same vein serve among those who want things instantaneously absent the time and honest work it takes to obtain. Essentially many today want in a microwave what is better accomplished in a slow-cooker or oven. Flavor, consistency and the finished product in all that you do is undoubtedly affected by the method you use to get the final result. Because God is time and his equation is on a different scale than ours we cannot measure our effectiveness based off of the duration of our expectations. Likewise, as it relates to relationship, we must be willing to dedicate this precious unit of measurement as a tool to build; time is to be spent studying, gleaning, being productive, and just being. In the state of being we are able to enjoy the presence of God and have our spirit renewed, replenished, and revived. As in a natural relationship we learn how to please those we love by studying what they like and dislike, watching their habits, tendencies and even shortcomings and learning what it takes to please them and make the whole relationship more productive as a whole. Thus, the more time you spend in the presence of God the closer you must become.

No relationship is fruitful when the efforts are one-sided. We must always be in a place to be attentive to the will of God, His Spirit, and His will in the Earth. A great part of our ability to be attentive is our gift to discern. When we tap into discernment, we are able to not only see and feel the heart and intentions of God, but we are able to intercede for others, open our being with regard to ourselves, and be a vessel to be used in a way that is tailored for that moment in time. Discernment is real time sensitivity to the spirit. We must remain in a place where our lives are never too loud to hear the small unction of the Holy Spirit or miss the moves that seem minuscule, but are mighty to the Kingdom of God. Don't ever lose your ability to be open and vulnerable to God; when we are susceptible to Him we are akin to clay where God has the ability to shape us, mold us, place us where he sees fit and use us over and over again for the glory of the Kingdom and the fulfillment of our destiny.

Unity

We must always be on one accord with the Spirit of God. As you can see, each principle ties in to the other, showing us how intentional our foundation with God must be to be effective. Unity is indicative of knowing the character and attributes of God and executing them in our daily walk. To be on one accord with Him we must walk in His image, believe in His statutes, live His Word, and be effective witnesses to the cause of Christ. We cannot preach or teach one way and live another or we are not in unity and our dissension with the body will manifest in the little fruit produced or the lack thereof altogether. There must be oneness of mind, body, soul, and spirit as it relates to the will of God so what our work & witness bring glory, not disdain, to the Body of Christ. Our unity must also entail that we are on the same page as God as it relates to our destiny otherwise we become productive worker bees busy but never actual accomplishing anything. We perform better doing what we are equipped to do rather than what we feel we need to do absent the skill or approval of our creator. At times what we want to do will fall apart merely because we are operating absent the will of God regardless of the task. We must stay in our lane.

Honesty

Transparency is essential to building the bridge in the relationship that we will need to travel back and forth across on the journey of life. Even in his ability to be omnipotent, omniscient, and omnipresent, we must remain in a state of transparency with God for ourselves and because an exchange of honesty keeps the lines of communication open and leaves the foundation open for truth to reside there as the cornerstone of the relationship. When we can be truthful with God even in our shortcomings he can use us because our honesty enables Him to work with us, on us, and through us as we come to the realization that absent Him we are nothing. When we otherwise fail to be open with God we bruise the heart of the relationship and it later damages trust opening us up to an inability to move forward in the relationship. Where there is no honesty, there is no trust, unity, or need to build moving forward. Without the cornerstone of trust, as the foundation is built upon, it's fall is inevitable and surely detrimental to all parties involved.

Communication

Communication goes beyond talking; it is rather an intimacy of sorts where we are able to be naked before God with our hopes, dreams, aspirations, fears, deficiencies and even our failures. The more we open up to God the more he reveals to us. We communicate through the monologue of prayer and the exchange of the Spirit as God speaks to us. One place where we fail in communication is we get frustrated when God doesn't speak to us. Many times He is speaking but we've chosen not to hear because its not what we wanted or expected, we fear to hear that it IS what we needed, or we fail to see his response in the signs that follow. One thing about communication in a relationship is that it must be fair — as much as we want to be honestly heard we must open ourselves to honestly listen to hear and not listen to respond. When we are willing to hear God without excuse mysteries are revealed to those He can trust to His voice. Communication is another cornerstone that is imperative because we cannot build with someone we don't trust to see us naked.

Trust

Do you believe without a doubt that God has your best interest as heart? This is a tough one because this is where our will tries to intermingle with God's divine will. In a relationship we must trust that our partner wants the very best for us even when the best seems like the farthest from what we ever desired or saw for ourselves. We have to believe that if we fail God will cover and restore us and should we lose our balance or fall backward that God will catch us and stand us upright again. Trust is hard because we tend to rely on our own strength and ultimately offend the intentions of the one with whom we share our life with, sending the message that they are not needed or that their actions are not indicative to the success or well-being of the relationship.

God will always have our best interests at heart. At times trusting God equals taking down, being unsure, doing it afraid and walking through the unknown. The best part is even in the times where we are not confident in what is to come we are reminded that we have an advocate and a savior who has vowed to never leave us or forsake us. Trust is the cornerstone that reminds us that we must mutually enable one another to do what is best for the relationship absent of judgment or failure to support; failure to trust will cause us to abandon the relationship out of fear regardless of what has been built in the past. An abandoned building is useful to no-one except it be restored and put to use again.

Vision

Vision goes hand in hand with trust and unity. The vision for where the relationship will go must be one that is of mutual agreement; we must trust God with the vision for our lives so much so that our unity with Him causes us to do it regardless of our inability to know the outcome. Where God gives vision, PROvision is often on the coattails to ensure we have what we need to succeed. There was once a saying by an author unknown that said 'God doesn't give a vision to match our budget, he gives vision to match our faith'. If we can accomplish it ourselves and absent any help from God it's not vision or faith because anything God gives is going to need Him coupled with our need to use our insight, not our eyesight. To use our natural eyes is to see things as they are but to use insight is to envision by faith what the destined outcome is and see it to fruition through no natural will or power of our own. God has a vision for your life; though there have been times for all of us where we are despondent, discouraged, distracted and detoured, His vision has been consistent. Our heartbeat is a reminder of the purpose within us to move forward, set goals, trust God and see the vision come to pass.

Love

Love is the cornerstone that completes the bottom of the foundation. Love is a combination of the above coupled with caring, empathy, wisdom and understanding. Love enables us to see one another as we are and yet through the eyes of love see one another at our purposed best all in the same glance. Love is not selfish but it seeks to please the other; it takes wisdom to truly love someone because you must be prescriptive in your approach and execution and understanding of what the individual needs are to ensure the receiving party is accepted and fulfilled. Love cannot be presumptuous nor can one afford to assume or you run the risk of what you offer being deficient and creating a void in the relationship. Love can be hard because depending on the need it can seem very lopsided like the see-seesaw that is often tipped in one or the other partner's favor. This is why love must always be patient and kind because it is often more well-ridden on a smooth road. As much as love is consistent there will be highs and lows as well. As much as we feel like we are giving to God, we have to mindful of all He has sacrificed for us and gives to us daily all out of love to ensure our basic survival needs are met.

Hope

Hope is the glimmer we find to hold on to, especially in the tough times, to give us something to look forward to. We will have those times where it seems like we are lost or hardly hanging on when hope seemingly comes out of nowhere and steps on the scene. Hope reminds us that we have a purpose and that we are capable of fulfilling what seems impossible. In the relationship hope restores those principles that are lost reminding us of the good times, so we can sail across the less than favorable times in search of brighter days. We need those dark days sometimes to remind us to appreciate the days we take for granted when it seems as if all things are working together for our good.

Compromise

The essentiality of compromise is often found close to its cohort in the dreaded submission. We often fail to embrace what we do not fully understand. Compromise is essential in the building blocks because in order for stability to be accomplished there will often be give and take dependent upon what is needed for either party at that time. Compromise sometimes entails us having to do things for our partner that we either would not normally do or do not want to do altogether, however, we do it because at that time it is necessary for them for acceptance, affirmation, and even adoration. We give of ourselves fully knowing that God will give to us at the time needed, sometimes outside of His own will, if it's something we are convinced we cannot go without. Compromise should never be something that endangers the health of the relationship nor cause either party to abandon moral compass or spiritual value.

Reciprocation

Reciprocation is necessary to have confidence in the fact that as much as what you need will be provided, you will in turn have what is necessary to give back to the relationship. God is not our sugar daddy, so we must not have a 'give me' mentality. We offer our gifts in time, talent, and treasure for His glory and the building of the kingdom, and he in turn equips us, blesses us and ensures all of our needs are met. We reciprocate by worshipping God in Spirit, truth and remaining in right relationship with His Word & will, fleeing and resisting the wiles, temptations, thoughts and acts the enemy may try to influence us to do.

Each principle in its individuality as well as the totality

has revealed to us how pivotal it is to know God on a deeper level. God is not the complex being many have made Him to be; yes He is full of mystery, revelation and thoughts of unknown depths accompanied by a will that cannot be fully comprehended but, he is also simple, loving, and has a language that those in close relationship can understand when we put the principles to work. We have enough people in the world still lost and trying to find their way; we have still more people not looking to be found and okay with being lost. Let's be the difference. Get to know God on a deeper level and open yourself to His vision for your life. One thing about the vision of God is that regardless of huge it may initially seem, its execution and purpose fits like a puzzle piece when you walk in to it. Remember that nothing will ever feel more right than obediently doing what you were created to do.

How is it that one not knowing who they are in life or in Christ can cause one to be dead in the pews? Sometimes we hold people accountable for us not knowing who we are. God can give your spiritual leader insight as to who you are or what you may need from them to fully get there but it is not the leader's responsibility alone to know who you are in Christ and get you there. That leader has to do that for themselves as it relates to them personally. We must stop taxing others with our responsibility. Them not knowing who you are is not holding you back; you not knowing who you are and not being is tune with God holds you back. You must know God for yourself and as admonished in Philippians 2:12, work out your own soul salvation with fear and trembling (meaning very carefully / cautiously). Additionally, you cannot be so enamored with "them" and how they are living, what they are doing, and condemning "them" to Hell, so much so, that you are neglecting your own spiritual walk.

When you know who you are, don't dumb it down for anybody. I spent years dumbing down and hiding because I allowed others to impose upon me who I was not instead of following the leading of God. Don't allow anyone to put you in a position, place or to operate a gift you are not graced for or called to because it will attract warfare you are not equipped to handle; furthermore, being in a place out of loyalty over calling can cause a harboring of resentment, when in fact you should not be there. The people on the front line of the battle are trained to be in the heat of the battle; those in the back are trained differently as are those in the middle. It's not to say that one position is better than the other because they are all needed, but it is obvious that there would be less casualties of war in the church if we'd stay where we are trained, gifted, called, and equipped to do. Staying in your own lane is sure to cause less accidents.

Lastly, you have a duty to become. Yes, that's a complete sentence. You were born for a purpose and there is no disclaimer before you were born or escape clause to get you out of it. We all have a destiny and a gift that only we can give to this Earth. If you fail to ask God who you are and what you are called to do, let me serve you notice: **avoidance doesn't excuse you from your destiny!** I've encountered many who are happy not seeking God for what they must do because they are living for themselves and merely not ready. The same people are in repetitive cycles, chasing happiness because they aren't connected to the source of joy, and waiting for the next great thing to happen to prove God is blessing them too, even in their disobedience. Grace and mercy must not be vehicles to ride from sin to sin or to keep seeing how far we can push God without punishment. Your life must not be a roulette table in Vegas, gambling and taking a chance where it lands when you either pay it big or flop and lose. God will hold us accountable for every deed and when we fail to complete our purpose. Every day you wake up is a chance to be better, do better and be who you are called to be, without excuse.

6

Opaque Transparency

Objects in mirror are closer than they appear is an often over-looked warning embossed on the bottom of most mirrors, a warning many take for granted. While a mirror shows us a reflection of what is there, it is up to us to see our truth, face it and walk in it. Mirrors are not kind, an object with a one way path of travel, having to see your reality staring back at you one faced with flaws, abrasions, breakouts, sadness, despair, joy, love, and pain. While we cannot change our reflection, we have the power to control how we look the next time and what we do in between time to improve upon what we see. The saying on the bottom of the mirror is a reminder that what you see, though appearing to be from a distance, is a palpable reality. How is this significant? If we can't face what we see, be real about what we choose to ignore or forget and own up to what we lack we will live a life of opaque transparency, which, at best, is oxymoronic in nature. This state of seeing is one of inconsistency and a reality that is clouded by what truly is and what one chooses to see, believe and even how they are perceived or received by others. You cannot outsmart the mirror any more than you can life; the only way to deal is to see what you see for what it is, not what you choose to make it become in the absence of realization and change.

Transparency is important because we cannot be who we were created to be if we cannot face who we are, how we got there, and how that path will lead us to our final destination. There is fear behind true transparency because of the unknown factors of possible judgement, ridicule, shame, an inability to forgive self and the possibility of exposure. One of the toughest things can be to take the chance of being exposed and left to fend for oneself to recover and survive. In spite of the unknown factors it is evident that the corporate church is in need of unadulterated transparency. Truth that is opaque in nature is not true at all, as the veil that covers it disables it from being full and complete. The corporate church cannot have complete transparency until the people (individual churches) face a reality check that will free others.

It is my belief that many die in the pews of churches that are more concerned with having the appearance of holiness, but denying the truth it takes to obtain, and the power thereof; still others die in the pews because they cannot meet the standard of holiness shown while struggling with their shortcomings and sin. Often times people want someone they can relate to who will understand their plight, perhaps having experienced it or something like it themselves at some point in time. Truth requires us to be honest with ourselves first, trusting that what is revealed is safe for us to self-absorb, righteously judge, repent, renounce and then go to God to be revived without "hiding" pieces of our reality from an omnipresent and omniscient God.

Psalm 37:37 admonishes us to mark the perfect man. Who is the perfect man? It is one who reveres God with his life and walks in the image of Christ, who we should all emulate. We are to take note of this person, not mock them. Matthew 5:48 advises us to "Be perfect, even as our Father in Heaven is perfect". We were born into sin and shaped in iniquity, so because we were born marred we will never be perfect but our life mission must be to strive for such and get as close as we can, not through appearance and works but through a consecrated life in Christ. As much as being created in the image of our Heavenly Father enables us to be a candidate for heaven, our nature by which we born into sin is a reality check that on the road to perfection we will not always do everything right. The key is not allowing where we have faltered to become a way of life. We must not use the excuse that we were "born" a certain way as if it disables us from change or living sanctified lives. Philippians 4:8 equips us with the tools to live a holy life by reminding us to think on the things that are lovely, pure, just, honest and of good report to keep us centered and focused on the goal at hand.

How does opaque transparency affect the church?

When people are so busy trying to be perceived as holy, without blemish and complete, the same judgement they refuse to face for themselves is often projected out on others. Perception, in the wrong hands, can be detrimental. We can be so busy looking a part that we do more damage than was ever intended. Misplaced judgement will lead others to shy away from their truth for fear of what exposure will bring. The Bible does not tell us not to judge per se, but to judge righteously and to be prepared to be judged by the same mete (measure) by which we have judged. To judge righteously is to expose the wound while facilitating healing with the provided tools for restoration. We are to ensure that as we judge it is not according to appearance (John 7:24) but by the universal standard, the Word of God, by which we must all measure up to. One cannot look holy and meet the requirements for holiness with that attribute alone. We can look well put together, polished, neat, well-dressed and even appear educated but perfection is not achieved by our outer appearance, but by the contents of the heart and truth of the Spirit.

Judgement has taken on a negative context because it has been used by some as a weapon; the word of God is not to be used as a bludgeoning tool, but rather as a guide to build us into the person God has created us to be. We are in a time where people who don't understand the nature of God refuse and shun judgement opting to be judged by God and God only. This perception of judgement is, in part, due to the misuse of judgement and a lack of understanding of who God is and what he represents. God is undoubtedly love, however, the same love that soothes, heals, builds and protects will also chasten, expose and bind up the wound that will sometimes bring more pain before healing. Most parents can relate to the fact that they've had to chastise their children because they love them and want them to be better and not make the same mistakes they once did; the love of God is as a parent to save the child from falling into destructive patterns and ways not like God that can jeopardize one's future. The reality is you don't want to be judged by God, especially if you don't have yourself together, as his judgement can render finality, whereas the judgement of people should be more constructive when given in love and received without offense.

When transparency is not clear, it doesn't just keep the person withholding in a box, but it affects those around them as well. A true testimony stopped belonging to you the day God exchanged your trial for triumph. God doesn't bring us through just to show us what He can do, especially if no one will ever know. God brings us through to help someone else. God gets the glory out of us much like juice comes out of a lemon or oil comes out of an olive. We will not like the process, beating, squeezing, crushing applying heat or pressure, but, it is after going through that we realize that what is inside of us is more precious than the outside image we seek to maintain and will be of greater benefit to those around us when we go through. Going through is hard. Facing what we have gone through can be even harder because we sometimes have to revisit the pain and remember what is felt like to be in that place to truly understand what healing looks like.

There are lives assigned to your transparency. There is a woman who is giving her body to multiple partners because she doesn't see or know she is worthy of more. Help her! There is a man who watched women be abused coming up and that is his normality. Help him find a better way! There is a woman who has had abortions due to shame, a moment of pleasure that left her with a gift she couldn't provide for and the pain is too great for her to bear. Help her! What about the woman beating herself up because she couldn't make her marriage work? She didn't just fail herself but she now must face the failure and ridicule from family, friends, and more. There are people struggling with their sexuality. Many are battling with suicide, depression, neglect, abandonment, rejection, sexual abuse.... HELP THEM! We must stop sitting pridefully, stifling the cries of aborted children, babies conceived out of wedlock covered by marriage, adulterous affairs, abuse in and out of the pulpit, marriages affronted by indifference and incompatibility and more.

God didn't bring you out to be selfish and enable you to sit around looking like you've always had it together and never made a mistake. Purporting an image of perfection does not help anyone including you, as your skeletons press on the door, while you do everything you can to mentally and physically keep them from falling out. If it is the truth that makes us free, and it is, then upholding an image laced with secrets means we are not truly free. Coming out with what you've been through can be hard but it's necessary because THEY need you and you deserve to be freed of the weight that you've carried too. They need someone like you did at your lowest point so that they can break through before they break down.

I admonish you to face you, no matter how tough that feat may be. No one wants to go back in the dark room because there is the underlying thought that it can suck you back in but if you never face it you cannot overcome it nor will you properly develop. You must ask God to help you see your past for what it is and then ask him for strength to overcome it and clarity to see the lessons you must learn in and through it. You see, as hard as it is to believe, there is always a good lesson in going through, but finding it can be likened to finding a needle in a haystack. I made excuses for being molested as a child and sexually violated as a teenager; I didn't face it, I found reasons to blame myself and my failure to deal with it affected relationships and the way I viewed everyone until I was freed from the trauma of the experience. I masked thoughts of suicide as mere discouragement because I didn't want people to know I was once weak enough to almost have given completely up. I stayed in unhappy relationships to avoid people seeing me as a failure and when one ended in divorce, I cringed at the thought of what people thought of me and even more, after yet another failure, I cringed at the thought of what I thought of me too. I could not help anyone until I faced me.

The Word of God brings about conviction when we yield to it; it's the enemy that dangles condemnation in front of us taunting us with the unknown and making us feel inadequate and unworthy of the love of God. When we are not open, honest and transparent we make those we should be help-ing as if we are the enemy because our façade of perfection hangs in front of them like a carrot to a rabbit teasing them with what they could never obtain, especially in the state they are in. It is only when we come to the realization that it is our process that brings glory to God not our perfection that we can be free to help someone else overcome. After freeing yourself, be intentional about helping someone who is dying to something they can recover from. Be the living proof that there is life after _____ !

7

No Fear Zone

FEAR. We've seen and heard the acronyms – False Evidence Appearing Real, Face Everything and Recover, Forgetting Everything About Reality... the list goes on and on and some make sense while most don't. I submit to you that fear is simply fear. Webster's Dictionary says fear is 1. an unpleasant of often strong emotion caused by anticipation of danger and accompanied by increased *autonomic activity* 2. Apprehension, worry or concern about what may happen.

Fear is an involuntary action to avoid the unknown which may not happen due to a prior personal experience or knowledge of one someone else has encountered. Why do I say fear is simply fear? Because fear is afraid of itself so much so that it hides and is empowered by regret, neglect, rejection, abandonment and is flanked by what if and has been. Fear is an evil spirit that seeks to paralyze you from achieving greatness and experience the fullness of God in your life as He so intended. Fear masks itself with distraction and rears its head as discouragement, deterrent and a disembodiment to detour you from the reality of who God has called you to be. I am stuck on the call of God because it is the very vain of our existence; because of Him we are and without Him we are not, cannot, do not and will amount to naught.

Fear reminds me of a costume contest. See, fear can survive alone, but it would be too easily recognized, so it dresses up as things it will likely never completely be for the sake of not being recognized as who it really is to wreak havoc in the lives of God's people. Fear is empowered when masked because without it, it's the one thing people would call out and expose. If you think about it, while it's not the only thing, fear is universal to the human race, in its original form, as a disgrace. It's a learned behavior that children cry when someone calls them afraid, as adolescents no one wants to be labeled as fearful because it's a time when they are coming in to their own and have an image to uphold and finally as adults admitting we are afraid of certain things is admitting failure so it is avoided. There are some who will tell you what they are obviously afraid of but won't admit the things that are hidden. It's important to dissect fear so we can recognize it, be freed from it and move forward.

Unresolved fear will manifest, like in the costume contest, as something it chooses to be recognized by. The point of the costume is not just to hide but to masquerade and act in a way you'd rather be associated with. Fear will manifest in many ways — just a few are avoidance, anger, resentment, distraction and rebellion. Before we get in to these, it is important to know that the only way to counteract fear is to admit it, face it and do afraid the very thing that is harboring the spirit of fear in your life and send it packing back to hell where the evil spirits belong!

Avoidance – Fear that is associated with past experiences will cause one to be afraid of ever undergoing that particular occurrence again. In this instance, fear will not only cause you to be leery of the unknown but will also replace your innermost needs and innate desires with decoy aspirations. When fear replaces your desires you can find yourself in an unrepentant state because you are only thinking of fulfilling the desires to avoid revisiting a place that once represented pain. *For example, a little girl dreams of marriage through childhood and into adolescence and adulthood. All she wants to be is a perfect wife and mother. She marries her prince charming and the marriage is one that ends in heartbreak, betrayal, pain, loss and abandonment. She is so hurt she feels punished by God in a sense because something that was right in his eyes failed so miserably. This failure doesn't just affect her but her relationship with God, family, and the fear of ever experiencing such hurt again causes her to avoid facing her feelings, seeking help, and to act in a way where eventually her desire for marriage is masked by everything else she is putting on top of it until the desire for marriage is gone altogether.* Avoidance seems acceptable because you don't go back to a place you think you're over but the reality is until that wound is completely opened, exposed, cleaned and stitched it will never fully heal and every attachment that reminds you of it will bring hurt and pain. You can avoid the wound but you will find constant reminders that you are not healed — whether or not you decide to deal with them is up to you.

Anger – unresolved fear can lead to anger, especially when one does not know how to deal with it. Why anger? Because the emotions lash out in a way to express what they cannot deal with. When one is angry they are usually masking feelings of inadequacy and insecurity but the mask of anger boosts their ego, makes them feel in control of what they won't admit and gives them a security because the wall that anger has built is not so easily taken down. Going through life with a wall as such can be detrimental because the emotional lows are very low to the point of abuse of self and others mentally, emotionally, spiritually and even physically, and the highs are insurmountable taking one to levels they can't soon come down from leaving a wake of destruction in it's path. Being the angry person is tough because it segues in to some of the other areas in which fear resides such as resentment from others, distraction from the real issue at hand and re- bellion from anyone and anything that represents better be- cause losing the anger means opening up to vulnerability and losing the security blanket of lashing out. Without that blan- ket people might actually find out that a person has feelings / struggles and once anger is uncovered fear will have to leave as well.

Resentment – this is a tough one because there is no middle ground with resentment because the foundation is not stable.

Fear leads to resentment because this person won't reveal how they truly feel due to fear of abandonment, confrontation, neglect or rejection. A failure to reveal how one truly feels leads to an assumption of abandonment of one's needs, wants and desires, and when those needs are not met a seed of antipathy is planted. There is no middle ground with resentment because you either resent a person for not being what you need or fear rears its head as offense because a person is working to be what you need but not on your terms and in such a way that you realize the past is not resolved and fear of revisiting that place breeds resentment with a person who unknowingly will eventually make you face what you'd rather avoid. There is no win with resentment, thus there comes a time when one must express how they feel to counteract ruining relationships that they realize they want and need, but don't know how to manage without fear of losing them altogether. Resentment is also bred when a person feels cornered into doing something as a result of an expectation that never agreed to; living up to hopes or rules that are imposed upon you creates undue pressure that implode in you or explode on them if not dealt with.

Distraction – Fear will do all that it takes to keep you from your destined place by any means necessary. We have to be mindful of the difference between a mere distraction and a destined detour because there is a fine line of dissimilarity. With a destined detour, we can be going the way we should but suddenly a curve ball comes our way that we can catch or swerve to avoid; swerving to avoid what we should catch and move forward with can be terrifying because one wrong move can alter your destined path. We must be careful here because often times, distractions don't look like distractions at all until it's too late — it can be a phone call, need from a friend, a game on the phone, a side conversation or visit, or a quick look at the television that culminates with the intention of watching one show turning into a season of episodes. How? Because distractions are so easy to fall for. The only way to counteract distractions is to pray against the spirit of distraction, ask God for strength to focus, endure and produce as well as stopping the distraction as soon as you recognize it and getting back on task. If the enemy can keep you distracted he can detour you from your destiny.

Rebellion – 1 Samuel 15:23 says "For rebellion is as the sin of witchcraft and stubbornness as bad as worshipping idols". Rebellion gives way to the ideology that we know what is best and in doing things our way, versus God's way will either yield better results or enable us to do what we want and still get rewarded in the end. A prime example of this is the journey of the children of Israel. After a mass exodus from slavery in Egypt generations of Israelites embark upon an 11 day journey that will lead to promise, abundance, provision and freedom; this journey does not take 11 days as it should but 40 years. While the Israelites had everything they needed for the journey, provision along the way and a leader to guide and teach them selfishness infiltrated the camp and discord and rebellion were birth in the midst of a people so close to the promise they could smell and touch it, but could not walk in and enjoy because they thought they knew better than God; rebellion caused them to question God, become distrustful of His intentions concerning them and ultimately cause many to die among them before taking ownership of their destiny.

How many times have we known what to do and how to do it but spent more time doubting our ability, questioning God, trying to convince God we know better or not doing anything we are destined to do all together and hoping for the best? Rebellion is rebellion no matter how you dress it up and it is rooted in the fear that IF this doesn't work out, IF I fail, IF they don't approve or IF I die in it that it would have been best to do it my way or stay in the prior situation I was in. Don't allow rebellion to rob you of the promised land. If God has promised it to you or given you the knowledge, plan or desire to do it, DO it because your promise is tied to your obedience.

The no fear zone is a state of mind. You must cast out fear by speaking to the very mountain you are afraid of, telling it where to go, and then doing what it takes to conquer it. We are human so this is not to say that in facing your fears that you won't have doubts or find yourself feeling as if you may fail or face that painful situation again. The only guarantee in facing your fears is that when you learn to trust God you won't have to do so alone; when you trust God in every situation you have access to his strength when you are weak so that failure is not only not an option but it will cease to rear it's ugly head because the enemy is no match for God. I challenge you that if that enemy sometimes feels like it is you, as it has been me, to ask God to show you yourself; ask God to show you every thought, desire, need, intention and area not like him and how to help you deal with it.

Don't give the enemy access to you in a zone cornered off by fear. While he has no rights to your destiny, he will make every effort to trespass on your territory to detour you; if you ever get to your destined place, you won't just walk in to a promise but you will unlock weapons of mass destruction in you that have the ability to nullify the kingdom of darkness (Hell). There are things that you will have to do afraid, sick, doubtful, nervous and unqualified. If you give God a yes he'll give you everything you need to see it to fruition. You have every right to deny access to the enemy and every thought and feeling that is not like God. Chase your destiny as if your life depends upon it… because it does.

8

Growing Pains: "Push or Die"

Many don't believe there should be any pain or trial, especially in God, because God is love. It is important to know that nothing we go through in God is to harm or kill us, but to build us, enable us to endure and to prepare us for the promise. Nearly everything in life goes through a process at some point to flourish and become what it was created to be. There is no choosing the process because if that were an option no one would choose trial and tribulation, and many would remain in a state of complacency as there would be nothing to strive from or change through. In this chapter particularly, let's deal with the joys and pains of childbirth. While a man cannot relate to the childbirth itself, he can identify with the process of growing in God and how the two are seemingly interrelated.

Childbirth is a beautiful thing. In an ideal situation a baby is conceived in love between a husband and wife after which the process of growing begins. While every situation is different, mothers carrying the child may experience miscarriage, bouts of nausea, vomiting, pain, difficulty sleeping, weight loss or weight gain, and a stretching of the body in ways once unimaginable to care for the growing gift that is soon to be birth. The husband may experience all or none of these sympathy symptoms depending on the individual situation. At some point in the pregnancy, the parents must decide who they will trust to help them deliver — a hospital, a doula or a midwife. The current trend is the midwife, whose focus is to provide one with the tools and controlled environment to result in a safe delivery without an adverse incident or invasive procedure.

In the beginning of pregnancy, upon finding out one is carrying life, it becomes about protecting the seed to ensure it is not lost; in the middle when the seed is "safe" it becomes about maintaining, and in the ending months or third trimester, the preparation mixed with anticipation, fear, and impatience is about ending one process to begin another. The process of pregnancy is delicate and vital because it is at this point that several things may occur: loss of life spontaneously because the body could not carry the seed, abortion or intentional abuse because the seed is not wanted by the carrier, or outside influences that know that the seed represents a promise and potential threat so fighting to remain pregnant to term becomes a daily battle. While carrying it is important to be mindful of the environment, who we surround ourselves by, what we eat (food and the Word of God) and who/where we choose to deliver. Spiritually, when we are entrusted with a gift, it is our duty to protect what we are carrying. 2 Timothy 1:14 (NIV) reads "Guard the *good deposit* entrusted to you — guard it with the help of the Holy Spirit who lives in us.

Childbirth is not typically without some measure of pain as the body prepares to defy the laws of nature to bring forth the miracle of life. Once the process of birthing begins it becomes more about managing what is without choice, because it's at a point where pain or no pain, the birth is inevitable. The birth is the most important part of the process to date because in the natural death passes over the woman statistically 9 times. We must not mistake for a moment that the enemy does not know what we are carrying or that he will allow us to birth it without trying to stop us. The pregnancy is long but even the most strenuous labor is relatively short compared to the term of the gestational period.

During the time of laboring there comes a time of being unsure, exhaustion, resistance and even wanting to give up because the pain is so great. Have you ever carried something so great in God that while you knew how huge this promise was, the labor almost took you out and made you give up? How about being in the process and not making it to the labor because you are worn out before you can get to the birth? Lamaze to the pregnant woman is the Holy Spirit and strength of God to the believer; in a time where so much is happening and emotions are running high we have to find a focus point, rely on the midwife, and breath through it. If we don't detach ourselves from the need to tap into our limited source of strength and the fear and weight that so easily besets us we run the risk of miscarrying the seed and killing ourselves.

There is a documentary about a woman in Morocco who once was pregnant but never gave birth. That happens at times, right? In this case she was married and looking forward to providing her husband with an heir in a time where a woman was considered "worthless" if she couldn't have a child. She carried the child nearly to term and went in to labor after a painful pregnancy. She made her way to the hospital for a Cesarean section and upon arrival became even more fearful of the procedure she was dreading, especially after watching someone else in her condition die. She went home still in labor, the baby kicking inside her, sending a signal that he was ready to come out. Her fear to birth kept her in her home where she went from a thriving pregnancy to a sudden silence; a baby once lively and ready to be birthed into the world suddenly stopped moving. The baby stopped kicking and passed away in the womb because she could not see beyond the birth to the promise; this mother, naive to the process, assumed God had removed the child and relieved her of the pending birth that she was so terrified of experiencing. After a short time, her husband and many noticed that she never birthed the child and she was eventually deemed barren, divorced, and ostracized due to the shame and ridicule of her inability to reproduce. Fast forward over fifty years later and she never had another child but she did have some adopted sons that looked after her. In her old age she began to get very sick and experience excruciating pain so she was taken to the hospital. After exams and multiple scans doctors determined she possibly had cancer and they needed to operate to remove the mass that had grown into her internal organs. Upon entering the abdominal cavity as doctors began to dissect her bodily tissues away from the mass they made a shocking discovery — the baby she never gave birth to was the mass that was now killing her. She carried the baby for over 55 years and admittedly stated that as time went on she thought the baby just went away, so she never told anyone that the fetus remained in her womb. After the mass was removed she was healthy again but the realization that she gave 55 years to fear was evident.

This story is powerful because this can and has been the life of some believers. It may even have been you, just for a shorter period of time. The only shame in it is choosing to carry and jeopardize what God has given you lest it kill you and the seed. There comes a time when we have to make a decision in the birthing process to push or die. Pushing is not comfortable, not easy and is certainly painful, but it is necessary. If a baby is not born naturally, the Cesarean section is an option, but can only be performed with your permission. Will you permit yourself to give birth or run away and carry the pain for the rest of your life? You see there is a pain that comes with not giving birth as well. There is a nagging reminder of what you could not or would not do especially as you see others coming forth with their gift.

It has not been 55 years but I have been the lady who would not birth. When I was initially inspired by God to write my first book I wrote it and became fearful and held on to the seed for years. I wrote enough for the seed to be conceived and maybe make it to the second trimester but I aborted it. I allowed the feelings no one knew I had as a child to contaminate my gift and smother my seed. As a child I always wanted to write and would climb up in the tree, write in my journal, read book after book and dream of becoming a Doctor and an Author. I didn't know how to move past feelings of inadequacy, low self-esteem, worthlessness and fear so I ate that and jeopardized what I was carrying due to the malnutrition of my spirituality. I miscarried that book at 20 years old. I always knew about that seed but didn't tell anyone I still carried it for fear of judgement and ridicule, while watching everyone else birth around me. 10 years later God inspired me to write the book you are reading.

It has taken me five years with the pregnancy but the birth has been almost immediate; as I fore stated, the pregnancy term is long but the strenuous labor is the part that is even more vital though a shorter period of time. I have wrestled with this book, dreaming of it, seeing it, hearing it audibly but never birthing it. I was reminded of the story of the woman all of those years ago and I decided I had to push or die because this book is taking up space in my womb where I should have released and been prepared to carry something else. How many babies (books) would I have birth if I hadn't allowed my fear to paralyze me from trying again or from admitting my fear and being delivered so I could produce? You see, the call to be fruitful and multiply goes beyond having babies, but is a call and a command to live a life that multiplies who you are what gift has given you in the Earth for His glory. Don't be like the children of Israel and travel around the same place for forty years in walking distance of the promise land but blinded by fear, rebellion, and passiveness. Birth.

PUSH OR DIE.

9

The Mask of Manipulation

The pews are not limited to people alone; interwoven amongst the souls the pews are metaphorically occupied by brokenness, rejection, manipulation, abuse in different forms (sexual, emotional and physical) and envy. The pews have become a hiding place, where especially in the absence of discernment and accountability, many have sat in the hospital sickly, overlooked, taken advantage of and worsening in their condition while the services, revivals, praise breaks and antics ensue around them. The church building, a beautiful edifice intended to be a place of worship, has in some instances become a den of thieves, liars and bleeding leaders who have contaminated the flock, refusing to hold others and themselves accountable and scattering sheep in the process. As one who loves, respects and holds the church in high regard, the aforementioned is simply unacceptable.

Manipulation often, like its distant relative fear, wears a mask, sneaking in disguised and undetected not showing its true colors until the havoc has been wreaked. Manipulation presents itself as a confidant, friend, trustworthy guide and partner infiltrating sacred places through erroneous teaching, tainted spiritual gifts — especially the prophetic — taking advantage of a lack if discernment or a vessel exhibiting doubt or vulnerability. To manipulate is to change the appearance or alter the functionality to fit the desired use while detracting from the intended purpose using control or influence; manipulation gains control first by exerting authority followed by planting seeds that eventually enable the manipulator to use their power over the "weaker vessel" to act in a way that further empowers the manipulator. No one person is special to a person who manipulates, when in fact, everyone is a pawn only useful for certain tasks or accomplishments before they are disposable.

Have you seen manipulation and control tear at the seams of your church, bringing about dissension? Have you been on the receiving end of manipulation and are not quite sure how you lost your footing? In order to fully understand both manipulation and control you must understand the origin of such. There is a name of a spirit that operates heavily in the area of inciting fear, envy, control and manipulation - Jezebel, first mentioned in the Bible in 1 Kings. In times past, Jezebel was often equated with a woman, promiscuous in nature, dressing provocatively as a woman of the night wearing red lipstick and long red nails, which could not be farther from the truth. Jezebel, under the influence of a powerful demonic spirit, was a queen who was married to King Ahab, was known for her beauty but soon became associated with her being a vessel used by evil bringing death & causing spiritual famine due to her greed, idol worship and deception into the land. Jezebel caused approximately ten million Hebrews to bow to Baal, forsake covenant with God, destroy the sacred altars and temples in the land and kill the Prophets of God. One woman / person operating under the guise of demonic spirits was noted to have corrupted an entire nation then and is still known to wreak havoc in the lives of people now.

Queen Jezebel had many favorable characteristics and traits which enabled her to gain initial entry before making her true intentions known; Jezebel was known for her beauty, independence, ambition, wit and inability to be controlled. The side of Jezebel that many didn't see initially was her divisive nature, embitterment towards others, misuse of authority and neglect of those she no longer had the need for. Jezebel's beauty was an open door for many to be mesmerized by her looks, soon finding out that she ulterior motives, albeit too late. Looks can be deceiving; thus, because we can often misconstrue what we see through our natural eyes we must always make a place for discernment, prayer and inspecting the fruit of those we encounter, serve, labor among and befriend. As beautiful as Jezebel was on the outside, she allowed her inner turmoil to cause her to act ugly, humiliating her husband King Ahab, manipulating him by playing on his fear of public embarrassment as he ruled that nation but had no true reign in his own home. King Ahab became a pawn to the devices of his mate, spineless when it came to accountability and ultimately meeting his own untimely death like that of Jezebel.

We have seen the works of the same spirit that dwelled with Jezebel in the church today. This foul spirit schemes and operates through both women and men who, due to their own insecurity, vainglory, jealousy or selfish desire to dominate others find themselves glorified puppets in the hands of the father of lies. In Revelation 2 (v. 19-29) a "Jezebel" like spirit is identified and exposed in it's favorite seat in the house, leadership; this is not to say that Jezebel only operates through leaders, but it is to say that this spirit is at its best when in any position to exert control over others, including but not limited to anyone from the pulpit to the door. In this passage in Revelation this spirit is found among the respectable men of God who outwardly preach and teach the love of God, seek to serve Him, influence others to do the same all while devising secretly in their hearts battling with lust and persuasion leading them to make decisions that are not honoring the God they profess to serve.

In both women and men, one of the primary spirits at work here is seduction. When we think of seduction, we tend to automatically equate it with sexuality, however, seduction is really a subduing of the senses by way of attracting and distracting. The spirit of seduction goes hand in hand with manipulation because one's vision is blurred and focus centered on something that may or may not be factual. The spirit of Jezebel operates in the church because many become seduced by charismatic expository lessons, false humility, the operation of spiritual gifts that may or may not glorify God in execution, etc. While distracted, behind the scenes abuse, adultery, lying, cheating, stealing, rejection and the like are running rampant.

We must not be so enamored that we don't move prayerfully, discerning, seeking God, looking for fruit that remains and trying the Spirit by the Spirit. The greatest of enemies to Jezebel wasn't a spiritual or natural enemy, army, or any persons who was against her actions. The Spirit of Jezebel is divisive in nature not fearing dissension, but rather more concerned that the true motives would be revealed and the very people turned against God or leadership in the church would see the error of their ways, repent and be restored — thus Jezebel's greatest enemies were the prophets and seers who could see, speak, and shift the atmosphere. Jezebel had seduced many but knew there were some that could not be so easily swayed, hence her mission to recruit others to senselessly murder the mouthpieces of God, the prophets.

If you are reading this ands have been under the influence of control, manipulation, rejection and the product thereof, you must be free. According to Hosea 4:6 we perish for the lack of knowledge, so now that you are informed you have a duty to live. In full transparency it is not easy to be freed from the grasp of a strong spirit as such; you may be labeled a renegade, fall into loneliness, depression, feel or be neglected, ostracized and more but, you will be free. The first weapon that we have the power to use to defeat the enemy is to see (vision), the second is to pray, the third to submit to God and the fourth to move according to God's plan for our life. So many sit in the pews stuck, unhappy, unsure and feeling as if they will fail God or be "doomed" if they move forward and detach from what is not healthy for them. We must know the difference between conviction and condemnation understanding that God will never lead you to anything that will draw you further from Him and the enemy will never tell you or influence you to do anything that will bring you closer to God.

You will not die if you choose to be free. You will succeed naturally and spiritually when you make the decision to free yourself. The stress, anxiety and sometimes depression that you feel is not of God. Family, friend or foe, you must go and serve where God ordains not where loyalty abides. Often times we stay and serve because we either want to prove others wrong or we become loyal to a fault dying in the process, because of fear of the unknown.

Many have set in the pews under abusive leadership that called it discipline, holiness and reverence. Still more have endured the pain of sexual abuse, immorality, spiritual fathers / mothers in incestuous relationships with their "offspring" yet they remain submitted because they respect their leadership, are bound by fear, marked by disgrace and made to believe stopping these acts are a disappointment to the leader and God. The pews are crying out for the depressed, hidden pregnancies and aborted babies, broken marriages, suicidal thoughts, legalism, rules, regulations, abused and more all in the name of a holiness that is not familiar to the God we serve. The pulpit cries for the leaders who bleed from the wounds caused by the sheep and other leaders, with no one to bandage their wounds. The sacred desk cries in agony for those who dare stand in a space of reverence while secretly committing every damnable act that defies accountability, responsibility and sanctification. No matter where you find yourself, you have a right to be free. It is only too late if you resign to the place that has kept you cuffed to your transgression; no matter the size of the mountain you can be free now!

My story

I found myself facing much of what was shared in this chapter on more than one occasion. I have served in places well that drained the very life out of me. I went to church out of obligation because I didn't want to get in trouble for not being there, but longed to feel the presence of God that it seemed those around me did. I sat there in silence depressed, anxious, dark, heavy, with what felt like the weight of the world on my shoulders. I found myself not having anywhere to lay my head, helped by others who lorded over me making me feel as if having nowhere was better than anywhere. I succumbed to pride to hide behind the hurt I felt so people wouldn't know that I was in need, or was not eating. I sat in a church having been sexually violated by two of the members there, yet told by the Pastor that "I needed to get over myself" while they laughed, taunted and even passed threatening notes to me while service was going on. I went through a painful divorce but felt too ashamed at having failed God and the expectations of the people to deal with my feelings in a healthy way. This is just a snippet, but guess what? It gets better.

I, thorough God, found myself. I found what God called me to do. I prayed and sought knowledge. I began to speak to every mountain that had amassed itself in my life, some due to my own permission and failure to remain accountable. The leaders who I knew were God-sent poured in to me and restored me mentally, emotionally and financially. Yes, I have been hurt, but my mountaintops outweighed every valley and taught me my worth as well as what not to accept. If I moved on, you can too. People will talk no matter what you say or do; there will always be opinions, however, the only will that matters if that of God. The safest place in the whole wide world is in the will of God.

Prayer

Father, we thank you for being God; we thank you for our life and another opportunity to examine ourselves and say yes. God we are so grateful for your love, kindness, mercy, grace and protection. Thank you for every person who, in faith, got this book, not for financial gain but because of a subconscious desire to be free. God we thank you that no matter where this reader has found themselves in these chapters, your grace is sufficient for every thorn they have faced. We bind every spirit not like you and loose your perfect peace, love, meekness, temperance and joy. I speak healing and breakthrough over the life of you reading and praying now; I pray that you find the strength to identify and the courage to move forward. We come against every plot, plan and device of the enemy to keep your children bound and command every foul spirit to loose their hold now and come out by fire and by force. Father thank you for your miraculous healing, delivering and restoring power. I speak to your finances and command them to be free. I speak to your mind and encourage you to take on the mind of Christ and evict every thought, intent and seed that has been planted that is not like God. In Jesus' name, amen!

You have everything you need in you to be free, to produce, to thrive and succeed. Never be bound again. No more masks. Go. Forgive. Love. Be free. LIVE!

Your Bones can Live!

Ezekiel was an exilic prophet who foresaw the fall of Jerusalem and was shown / able to experience the restoration that followed. Ezekiel 37 is a powerful passage in the Bible about Ezekiel, sitting in an open vision seeing the current and prophetic state of Israel. In this vision God is guiding Ezekiel through what he sees. Initially, in verses 1-2, all the prophet sees is a desolate place full of bones; there is no sign of life and then bones are no longer connected or resembling anything of hope. In verse 3, God asks Ezekiel if the bones can live, as to ask if he has faith that this situation can change, to which he responds to God that only he would know if that were possible. Sometimes as we are going through in life and looking at it from the outside in our mortality it is hard to see how we will ever come out, live through what we are in the middle of, or ever be restored. We walked through many of the situations that have left a lot us as dry bones in the valley, worn down, without life and essentially hopeless. I submit to you that with God life is always an option, in the toughest of situations, if only we'd trust Him and believe.

Ezekiel is challenged by the Lord to prophesy to the bones and as he does the bones began to rattle and stand up, get connected and became covered with flesh. Ezekiel is charged to prophesy again that breath would come into the newly formed bodies because existing was not enough. As breath came into the beings a mighty army was formed and they were great. These bones are you and I. They are the people that sit next to you in the pews day after day and Sunday after Sunday. These bones are the people hurt by someone in the church and now sitting at home because they have equated God with what has happened and given up on spirituality by way of relationship. These bones are every person who has become lost in their gift and calling, fallen prey to the shadows, or overcome by the limelight and lost sight of ministry.

The beautiful part about this life is that as long as we have breath in our bodies, we may feel dried and dead in the valley, but our purpose is very much alive. You that are reading, I command you to live. Forgive that person that may never be sorry. Step out afraid and write the book. Be obedient to the ministry with all humility because lives depend on what God has imparted in you. Seek God for deliverance from what has you bound. Leave the drugs and alcohol you are using to cope and ask God for the strength to deal with what you are medicating so that you can be whole. Some don't medicate with alcohol or drugs but they are in the pews with scars under those beautiful clothes where they have mutilated themselves; even more are going home to pornography ashamed of the struggle with lust and perversion that they don't know how to rid themselves of.

We all get lost at some point, some longer than others, but just as Ezekiel prophesied to the bones, encourage yourself and command yourself to live. Come forth and be as great as you were created to be. As we journeyed chapter through chapter I pray that you not only saw yourself in the pages situationally, but that you also found the strength and encouragement to know that you don't have to stay in a state of defeat no matter what got you there. You are great. You are called. You are purposed. You have a destiny and no one or anything can take that from you. All that you have gone through is a sign that your very presence threatens the enemy; don't settle for being a threat that never fulfills its purpose, but become the spiritual weapon of mass destruction to the enemy's camp. Why? There are people dead in the pews now and more will come; someone will have to show them how to live and move forward.

LIVE.

CPSIA information can be obtained
at www.ICGtesting.com
Printed in the USA
LVHW051252100221
678898LV00003B/320